FORWARD/COMMENTARY

This book consists of the testimony of respected cyber experts at a hearing of the House Armed Services Committee on March 1, 2017. The witnesses provide sobering insight into the extent of the cybersecurity threats facing our nation today. The witnesses discuss the policies that got us to where we are today, and possible changes in policy that could serve to bolster our computer network defenses against cyber-attacks in the future. In their testimony we are told of the multiple vectors for cyber-attacks from Russia, China, North Korea, Iran and non-state actors. The book includes the full written statements submitted by the witnesses as well as the responses to questions submitted by House Committee members post-hearing.

While most of the books we publish focus on the nuts and bolts of cybersecurity, this is the first book we've published to discuss a subject most techies are uncomfortable discussing–policy. If we are to be successful at preventing cyber-attacks, we must bring the techies into the policy conversation because inevitably these are the folks that implement policy. The more input they provide, the better chance we have of implementing an effective cybersecurity defense.

Cybersecurity policies cover a wide range of topics that must be designed to work together to produce a holistic approach to cybersecurity if we are to be successful.

Why buy a book you can download for free?

Some books are available only in electronic media. We print the larger books so you don't have to. Some online books are hard to find and many citizens don't even know they exist. We feel it's important that the opinions expressed by the cybersecurity community are widely distributed.

We at 4th Watch Books are also publishing this book so U.S. citizens gain insight into the workings of the Government and the considerable effort public servants put forth to keep our country safe. Congress gets a lot of bad press, but through it all, they diligently work through the really difficult problems, day in and day out. It's a thankless job and seldom do they get a pat on the back. Having worked for the Government for over 30 years, I have seen how hard members of Congress (and Federal employees) work and hope you too will appreciate their dedicated service to the nation.

Luis Ayala, Publisher

CyberSecurity Standards Library™

Get a Complete Library of Over 300 Cybersecurity Standards on 1 Convenient DVD!

The **4th Watch CyberSecurity Standards Library** is a DVD disc that puts over 300 current and archived cybersecurity standards from NIST, DOD, DHS, CNSS and NERC at your fingertips! Many of these cybersecurity standards are hard to find and we included the current version and a previous version for many of them. The DVD includes four books written by Luis Ayala: **The Cyber Dictionary, Cybersecurity Standards, Cyber-Security Glossary of Building Hacks and Cyber-Attacks**, and **Cyber-Physical Attack Defenses: Preventing Damage to Buildings and Utilities**.

- ✓ DVD includes many Hard-to-find Cybersecurity Standards - some still in Draft.
- ✓ Docs are organized by source and listed numerically so each standard is easy to locate.
- ✓ The listing of standards on the DVD includes an abstract of the subject, and date issued.
- ✓ PDF format for use on PC, Mac, eReaders, or tablets.
- ✓ No need for WiFi / Internet.
- ✓ Save countless hours of searching and downloading.
- ✓ Carry in a briefcase - terrific for travel.

4th Watch Publishing is releasing the CyberSecurity Standards Library DVD to make it easier for you to access the tools you need to ensure the security of your computer networks and SCADA systems. We also publish many of these standards on demand so you don't need to waste valuable time searching for the latest version of a standard, printing hundreds of pages and punching holes so they can go in a three-ring binder. **Order on Amazon.com**

The DVD works on PC and Mac with the standards in PDF format. To view the CyberSecurity Standards Library on the DVD, a computer with a DVD drive is required. The most current version of your internet browser, at least 2GB of RAM, and current version of Adobe Reader is recommended. (Compatible browsers include Internet Explorer 8+, Mozilla Firefox 4+, Apple Safari 5+, Google Chrome 15+)

CYBER WARFARE IN THE 21ST CENTURY: THREATS, CHALLENGES, AND OPPORTUNITIES

COMMITTEE ON ARMED SERVICES HOUSE OF REPRESENTATIVES

ONE HUNDRED FIFTEENTH CONGRESS

FIRST SESSION

HEARING HELD MARCH 1, 2017

U.S. GOVERNMENT PUBLISHING OFFICE

24–680

WASHINGTON : 2017

COMMITTEE ON ARMED SERVICES

ONE HUNDRED FIFTEENTH CONGRESS

WILLIAM M. "MAC" THORNBERRY, Texas, *Chairman*

WALTER B. JONES, North Carolina
JOE WILSON, South Carolina
FRANK A. LOBIONDO, New Jersey
ROB BISHOP, Utah
MICHAEL R. TURNER, Ohio
MIKE ROGERS, Alabama
TRENT FRANKS, Arizona
BILL SHUSTER, Pennsylvania
K. MICHAEL CONAWAY, Texas
DOUG LAMBORN, Colorado
ROBERT J. WITTMAN, Virginia
DUNCAN HUNTER, California
MIKE COFFMAN, Colorado
VICKY HARTZLER, Missouri
AUSTIN SCOTT, Georgia
MO BROOKS, Alabama
PAUL COOK, California
JIM BRIDENSTINE, Oklahoma
BRAD R. WENSTRUP, Ohio
BRADLEY BYRNE, Alabama
SAM GRAVES, Missouri
ELISE M. STEFANIK, New York
MARTHA MCSALLY, Arizona
STEPHEN KNIGHT, California
STEVE RUSSELL, Oklahoma
SCOTT DESJARLAIS, Tennessee
RALPH LEE ABRAHAM, Louisiana
TRENT KELLY, Mississippi
MATT GAETZ, Florida
DON BACON, Nebraska JIM BANKS, Indiana
LIZ CHENEY, Wyoming

MIKE GALLAGHER, Wisconsin ADAM
SMITH, Washington
ROBERT A. BRADY, Pennsylvania
SUSAN A. DAVIS, California
JAMES R. LANGEVIN, Rhode Island
RICK LARSEN, Washington
JIM COOPER, Tennessee
MADELEINE Z. BORDALLO, Guam
JOE COURTNEY, Connecticut
NIKI TSONGAS, Massachusetts
JOHN GARAMENDI, California
JACKIE SPEIER, California
MARC A. VEASEY, Texas
TULSI GABBARD, Hawaii
BETO O'ROURKE, Texas
DONALD NORCROSS, New Jersey
RUBEN GALLEGO, Arizona
SETH MOULTON, Massachusetts
COLLEEN HANABUSA, Hawaii
CAROL SHEA–PORTER, New Hampshire
JACKY ROSEN, Nevada
A. DONALD MCEACHIN, Virginia
SALUD O. CARBAJAL, California
ANTHONY G. BROWN, Maryland
STEPHANIE N. MURPHY, Florida
RO KHANNA, California
TOM O'HALLERAN, Arizona
THOMAS R. SUOZZI, New York
(Vacancy)

ROBERT L. SIMMONS II, *Staff Director*
KEVIN GATES, *Professional Staff Member*
LINDSAY KAVANAUGH, *Professional Staff Member*
NEVE SCHADLER, *Clerk*

CONTENTS

Page

STATEMENTS PRESENTED BY MEMBERS OF CONGRESS

WITNESSES

APPENDIX

DOCUMENTS SUBMITTED FOR THE RECORD:
    [There were no Documents submitted.]

WITNESS RESPONSES TO QUESTIONS ASKED DURING THE HEARING:
    [There were no Questions submitted during the hearing.]

CYBER WARFARE IN THE 21ST CENTURY: THREATS, CHALLENGES, AND OPPORTUNITIES

––––––––

HOUSE OF REPRESENTATIVES,
COMMITTEE ON ARMED SERVICES,
Washington, DC, Wednesday, March 1, 2017.

The committee met, pursuant to call, at 10:03 a.m., in room 2118, Rayburn House Office Building, Hon. William M. "Mac" Thornberry (chairman of the committee) presiding.

OPENING STATEMENT OF HON. WILLIAM M. "MAC" THORNBERRY, A REPRESENTATIVE FROM TEXAS, CHAIRMAN, COMMITTEE ON ARMED SERVICES

The CHAIRMAN. The committee will come to order. The committee meets today to explore "Cyber Warfare in the 21st Century: Threats, Challenges, and Opportunities." Needless to say, it is a big complex topic that is at the heart of much of American national security today and will be even more so in the future.

One of those internet quotes attributed to Albert Einstein says: Given one hour to save the planet, I would spend 55 minutes understanding the problem and 5 minutes resolving it.

Well, whether Einstein really said something like that or not, I think the point rings true that much of our challenge in cyber is understanding the problem. As we have seen in recent years, cyber is being used by both nation-states and nonstate actors in ways that challenge our traditional notions of what is war. It is being used to destroy, to steal, and to influence.

Cyber is a domain of warfare in itself, but its technologies also undergird most all of our defense efforts. It helps make us the strongest military in the world, and it also presents a vulnerability, which adversaries are looking to exploit.

And what is true for our military is also true for our society. Those technologies offer great opportunity but are also a vulnerability that must be defended. And when it comes to things that must be defended, we often turn to the United States military.

I am very grateful to all the members who came back to Washington early this week to spend our yearly retreat at Fort Meade focusing on this issue. Our witnesses today will also help us advance our thinking and hopefully help lead us to find the right questions so that we can work together to find the right answers.

I would yield to the ranking member for any comments he would like to make.

STATEMENT OF HON. ADAM SMITH, A REPRESENTATIVE FROM WASHINGTON, RANKING MEMBER, COMMITTEE ON ARMED SERVICES

Mr. SMITH. Thank you, Mr. Chairman. I appreciate you holding this hearing on this very important topic, and it is one that I guess we are probably going to spend more than 55 minutes trying to figure out the problem, unfortunately. It is very complicated. You know, the first thing we have to figure out is how, you know, best and better to protect our networks, both within government and those private sector groups that we come into contact with the government. We have that problem on the Armed Services Committee with a lot of the defense contractors that have sensitive information within their cyber domain that we have to figure out how to protect.

And we still don't really have a comprehensive strategy for how to do that. That is part of the problem. And the other part is, as cyber is increasingly used for active warfare, what is our policy on that? If we are attacked through cyber, what is an appropriate response?

We saw that with the Russian attacks on the DNC [Democratic National Committee]. You know, the President responded. It took a long time because we really don't have a set policy on what is a proportional and appropriate response to a given cyber attack, which we need to figure out.

And then, lastly, how do we use it as an offensive weapon? Certainly our enemies are using it. ISIS [Islamic State of Iraq and Syria] is using it very effectively to spread their message and recruit. You know, and we have seen Russia use it in a variety of different formats. We have suspicions of others using it as well.

What should we do, from an offensive standpoint, to use cyber to cause problems for our enemies and advance our interests? So those are the three questions I am most interested in learning more about.

I apologize; I actually have to leave early from this hearing. But certainly I will study the remarks of our witnesses, and I know the panel will benefit from the discussion.

I thank the chairman for holding this hearing, and I yield back.

The CHAIRMAN. I thank the gentleman.

Again, let me thank each of our witnesses for taking the time to be here.

We have Dr. Peter Singer, strategist and senior fellow at New America Foundation, among others things, author of ''Wired for War'' and ''Ghost Fleet''; Dr. Martin Libicki, professor at the U.S. Naval Academy and adjunct management scientist at the RAND Corporation; and Mr. Jay Healey, nonresident senior fellow for the Cyber Statecraft Initiative at the Atlantic Council.

Thank you all for being here. Without objection, your full written statement will be made part of the record, and we would be pleased to hear any oral comments you would like to make at this point. Dr. Singer, we will start with you.

STATEMENT OF PETER SINGER, STRATEGIST AND SENIOR FELLOW, NEW AMERICA FOUNDATION

Dr. SINGER. Chairman Thornberry and Ranking Member Smith, members of the committee, it is an honor to speak at this important discussion today designed to reboot the cybersecurity conversation. It is all the more needed as the United States was recently the victim of what was arguably the most important cyber attack campaign in history. Hackers reported as working on behalf of the Russian Government have attacked a wide variety of American citizens and institutions. They include political organizations of both parties, the Republican National Committee and the Democratic National Committee, as well as prominent Democrat and Republican leaders, as well as civil society groups like various American universities and academic research programs.

These attacks started years back, but it continued after the 2016 election. They have been reported as hitting clearly government sites, like the Pentagon's email system, as well as clearly private networks, like U.S. banks. They have also been reported as targeting a wide variety of American allies ranging from government, military, and civilian targets, and states that range from Norway to the United Kingdom, as well as now trying to influence upcoming elections in Germany, France, and the Netherlands.

While Vladimir Putin has denied the existence of this campaign, its activities have been identified by groups that include all the different agencies of the U.S. intelligence community, the FBI [Federal Bureau of Investigation], and in statements by both the prior and present U.S. President. This campaign has also been well-established by the marketplace. Five different well-regarded cybersecurity firms have identified it.

This campaign is not a cyber war of the kind that is often envisioned with power grids going down and fiery cyber Pearl Harbors. Instead, it is a competition more akin to the Cold War's predigital battles that crossed influence operations with espionage and subversion.

However, while Russia's attacks are the most notable events in cybersecurity in the last year, unlike in the Cold War, our strategy must recognize they are only one aspect of a larger threat landscape. In cyberspace, the malevolent actors presently engaged in attacks on U.S. persons and institutions range from criminals who are stealing personal information or holding ransom valuable corporate data—although here too there is a prominent Russian link with reportedly 75 percent of ransomware coming from Russian- speaking parts of the online criminal underground—to governments, like China, which have been accused of large-scale intellectual property theft, as well as breaking into government databases like the OPM [Office of Personnel Management] in the cyber version of traditional espionage.

And, finally, our strategy must face that all of this ongoing activity must account for the risk of an actual cyber war, the activities that would occur in outright conflict, including cyber attacks to cause physical damage.

So what can be done to defend America in this challenging realm? In my written testimony, I submitted a series of 30 actions that can be taken by the Congress to raise cybersecurity. Notably, in reflecting the nature of this nonpartisan realm, the overall strategy in each of the proposed 30 measures are designed to be amenable to and implementable by the leaders of both parties.

I have submitted this strategy for the record, which I hope will be a useful resource to you and your staff in your important work ahead. Rather than restating in detail, I would note that it involves three core elements.

First, activities that can be taken to restore deterrence, from making key new investments in training, cutting-edge technology like artificial intelligence [AI], and organizational changes in our Defense Department approach, including disentangling CYBERCOM [Cyber Command] and the NSA [National Security Agency], to utilizing all our tools of power to better influence current and future adversary thinking in the wake of Russia's attack, most especially by turning sanctions into law and strengthening them.

Second, actions to raise resilience, our ability to shake off attacks and thus create what is known as deterrence by denial, where we are not only better protected but adversaries gain less and are thus less incentivized to attack. Importantly, a strategic effort to raise U.S. resilience would be a useful investment against any type of attack or attacker.

The steps that can be taken by Congress here range from measures to better utilize Pentagon buying power to oversight on the implementation of industry best practices in the government. They also include innovative means to deal with our cybersecurity human resource challenge, from supporting better pipelines into government and the military and better organizing the wealth of talent that lies outside of government in the military and Reserves, such as through the creation of a program akin to Estonia's world- respected approaches to societal resilience.

The final tract looks at the broader challenge we face in a world of social media and online influence operations. Here, too, there are a range of suggested congressional actions, including enhancing cybersecurity information sharing among likely U.S. political targets, raising the ability of the U.S. military to better utilize social media and integrate it into our own training environments, and supporting the recreation of the Active Measures Working Group, an interagency Cold War program designed to debunk foreign propaganda and limit the impact of lies spread by what the Soviets aptly called ''useful idiots.''

In conclusion, we must recognize that, for as long as we use the internet, adversaries like Putin's Russia and many others will seek to exploit this technology and our dependence on it in realms that range from politics to business to warfare itself. In response, the United States can build a new set of approaches to deliver true cybersecurity, aiming to better protect ourselves while reshaping adversary attitudes and options, or we can continue to be a victim.
Thank you.

[The prepared statement of Dr. Singer can be found in the Appendix on page 47.]
The CHAIRMAN. Thank you. Dr. Libicki.

STATEMENT OF MARTIN C. LIBICKI, PROFESSOR, U.S. NAVAL ACADEMY, AND ADJUNCT MANAGEMENT SCIENTIST, RAND CORPORATION

Dr. LIBICKI. Good morning, Chairman Thornberry, Ranking Member Smith, and the distinguished members of the committee. My name is Martin Libicki, the Maryellen and Richard Keyser Chair of Cybersecurity Studies at the Naval Academy and an adjunct at RAND. The views expressed are my own.

Two years ago, Admiral Rogers asked Congress to support an increase in his ability to carry out cyber attacks so that the United States could deter cyber attacks on it, but would strength alone suffice? Our deterrence capability has at least four prerequisites.

First, we must be able to attribute cyber attacks in order to punish the correct party and convince others that we are acting justifiably.

Second, we must communicate our thresholds. What actions will lead to reprisals?

Third, we need credibility so that others believe that punishment will in fact follow crossing such thresholds.

Fourth, we need the capability to carry out reprisals.

Of the four prerequisites, it is U.S. capability that is least in doubt. Any country credited with Stuxnet and the operations that Snowden leaked has demonstrated an impressive capability. It is the other three prerequisites that need attention.

Attribution, to be fair, has improved considerably over the past 10 years, but the same cannot always be said about the U.S. ability or willingness to prove that its attribution is correct. After the Sony attack, the FBI's public statement devoted just 140 words to justifying its attribution, and the public case that Russia carried out the DNC hack is even more problematic.

Credibility remains an issue. Although the United States did retaliate against North Korea for the Sony attack and Russia for the DNC hack, the reprisals that have been made public, mostly sanctions, were not the sort that would induce fear in others.

That leaves the issue of thresholds, which gets the least attention. What cyber attacks merit cranking up the machinery of U.S. retaliation for and thereby potentially altering the U.S. relationship with another country, especially when cyber attacks can vary so much from a momentary network disruption to a major catastrophe? Not everything that we might call a cyber attack is actionable.

By contrast, even the smallest nuclear weapon on U.S. soil was obviously actionable. Finding a tractable threshold is not a problem easily solved. So let's consider some candidates.

Should something be actionable if it violates the Computer Fraud and Abuse Act? Well, there are three problems. First, using a national law as an international red line sets a precedent easily abused by countries that, for instance, criminalize free speech.

Second, this act is violated literally on millions of occasions, pretty much every time a computer is turned into a zombie.

Third, such a law makes cyber espionage an actionable act, but this is something that the United States carries out all the time.

Well, is something actionable, as one Assistant Secretary of Defense argued, if it is among the top 2 percent of all attacks? Here the problem is that cyber attacks have no minimum. So it is very difficult to define the set and, thus, very difficult to define 2 percent of the set.

Okay. Should everything that affects the U.S. critical infrastructure be actionable? Supposedly we know what is and is not part of the U.S. critical infrastructure. But then we have attacks that make us change our mind. For instance, a number of folks said the attack on Sony was an attack on the critical infrastructure, and after the attack on the DNC, we reconsidered the election—the voting machinery in this country, and we reclassified it as part of the critical infrastructure.

Well, do the laws of armed conflict, or LOAC, provide a good dividing line? Well, unfortunately, LOAC kicks in only when something is broken or someone is hurt, and in cyberspace, damage has occurred twice and death not at all. An attack that bankrupts a firm, by contrast, would not be actionable by LOAC. Worse, LOAC fosters the notion that a cyber attack, like a physical attack, is unacceptable behavior for countries, while cyber espionage, like traditional espionage, is something countries do. But the United States does not accept all cyber espionage. It successfully pressed China to stop its economic cyber espionage.

If the data taken from OPM had been sold into the black markets, the United States would doubtlessly have raised very strong objection to China, and the DNC hack was actually cyber espionage. If the Russians had taken what they took in-house rather than post it online, there likely would have been no U.S. response.

My bottom line is this: deterrence introduces multiple issues that need far more careful attention than they have received to date. Being strong is necessary, but it is not sufficient, and until we have a firmer basis for setting thresholds, we may have to limit reprisals to obviously actionable attacks while using the less obvious ones as markers for what we would react to next time.

I appreciate the opportunity to discuss this important topic, and I look forward to your questions.

[The prepared statement of Dr. Libicki can be found in the Appendix on page 60.] The CHAIRMAN. Thank you. Mr. Healey.

STATEMENT OF JASON HEALEY, NONRESIDENT SENIOR FELLOW, CYBER STATECRAFT INITIATIVE, ATLANTIC COUNCIL

Mr. HEALEY. Good morning, Chairman Thornberry, Ranking Member Smith, distinguished members of the committee. I am really humbled to be in front of you today. I will jump right to the heart of my comments on cyber conflict where several issues stand out.

First, what isn't a problem? Attribution, as my colleagues have pointed out, is not nearly the challenge that it used to be, as analysts at private sector companies and the U.S. Government have made tremendous gains determining which nations are behind cyber attacks.

Second, what is different in cyber compared to conventional conflict? I believe it is not hazy borders or operating at network speeds or the other things that you might have heard that is most different, but in fact the role of the private sector. America's cyber power is not at Fort Meade. No, the center of U.S. cyber power is instead in Silicon Valley, in Route 128 in Boston, at Redmond, Washington, and in all of your districts where Americans are creating and maintaining cyberspace and can bend it if they need to.

Third, what didn't we see coming? In the wake of the 1991 Gulf War, we in the military were eager to study information operations, including propaganda and influence, which are now some of our adversaries' primary weapons against us. Yet, in the time since, we have become so enamored of the cyber, we have forgotten critical lessons of information operations from that time.

Fourth, what might we have most wrong? Simply, deterrence and coercion. Previous testimony to this House made it clear there was an electronic Pearl Harbor waiting to happen. Well, that was in June 1991. So we have been fretting about an electronic Pearl Harbor for 25 of the 75 years since the actual Pearl Harbor. Cyber deterrence above the threshold of death and destruction not just is working but works pretty much like traditional deterrence. Where deterrence is not working, of course, is in the gray area between peace and war, where all major cyber powers are enjoying a free-for-all.

We should not kid ourselves. In that gray zone, the United States is throwing as well as taking punches, and deterrence works very differently if your adversary is certain they are striking back, not first. In fact, I believe cyber may be the most escalatory kind of conflict we have ever encountered. Because of this, any exercise in cyber deterrence must be thought of as an experiment. Some of our experiments will work; some won't. So we must be cautious, attentive to the evidence, and willing to learn.

So my first recommendation is that a new set of cyber influence teams might quickly be trained and folded into the Cyber Mission Force at Fort Meade working alongside cyber and area studies experts there.

Second, I continue to advocate splitting the leadership of NSA and Cyber Command. Imagine if the Commander of U.S. Pacific Command were the leading source of information on the China military threat, negotiated with U.S. companies dealing with China, ran the best funded China-oriented bureaucracies, was involved in intelligence operations and military planning against China, and could decide what information on China was classified or not. Sometimes two heads and two hats are more American than one.

Third, the best use of government resources is to reinforce those doing the best work already. Our critical infrastructure companies are on the front lines and, together with major vendors and cybersecurity companies, have far more defensive capabilities than our military. Grants to the nonprofit associations that are knitting these operations together can give massive bang for the buck.

Lastly, I would like to leave you with a question to consider asking others in testimony in the future: What do you believe will be the dominant form of cyber conflict in 10 years? The Pentagon seems to have a healthy set of cyber requirements but not many views of what cyber conflict might be like as they do in the land, sea, air, or space.

For example, I am sure the chief of staff of the Air Force can give you many reasons on why he sees future air conflict and why a long-range strike bomber is the answer to succeeding in many of those kinds of conflicts. What do we think the future of cyber conflict might be like that will justify the requirements that the Pentagon is asking for?

In closing, I would like to mention that on 16 and 17 March, 48 student teams, including from many of your districts or your alma mater, including the Air Force Academy, Brown, and the Universities of South Alabama and Maryland, College Park, will compete in the Cyber 9/12 Student Challenge. This competition prepares students to tackle exactly the same sort of challenges about which my colleagues and I are testifying before you today. If you or your staff are available to observe, judge, or provide remarks, the student teams would greatly benefit. Thank you for your time.

[The prepared statement of Mr. Healey can be found in the Appendix on page 71.] The CHAIRMAN. Thank you.

As we notified all members, Mr. Smith and I agreed that, for the purpose of this hearing, we would start out by going in reverse seniority order for those members who were here at the time of the gavel and then go in order that members entered the room, like we usually do.

I also want to remind members that this afternoon the Emerging Threats and Capabilities Subcommittee is holding a classified quarterly update on cyber operations to which all members of the committee are invited.

And at this point, I would like to yield my 5 minutes to the chair of that subcommittee, Ms. Stefanik.

Ms. STEFANIK. Thank you, Mr. Chairman.

I have two questions. The first is broad. What aspects of the previous administration's cyber policy should we keep and what should we rethink? I will start with Mr. Healey and move down the line.

Mr. HEALEY. Thank you very much, Chairwoman, Ms. Stefanik.

The previous administration got a lot of runs across the plate, but they weren't really swinging for the fence. So they had a lot of small—they were playing small ball. And so there weren't that many things that really angered me that much about what they did.

One that I think we should absolutely keep, because I think the private sector should be the supported command, not the supporting command, I am a big fan of the work that they had done on the vulnerabilities equities process. This is the process by which if the U.S. Government discovers vulnerabilities, especially in U.S. IT [information technology] products, that the default is to tell the vendors on that, and if they keep it, for example, at Fort Meade, that they have a risk-mitigation strategy so that, if it does become public, that they can respond most quickly. The work that they did on that was very important. That actually dates back to CNCI [Comprehensive National Cybersecurity Initiative] in the previous administration, but I think that is certainly worth keeping.

To change: I certainly hope that the U.S. Government can do better on its own cybersecurity systems. It looks like the new administration might be doing better on this with more of a role for the Office of Management and Budget as well as more shared services, that is, more cloud. I also think we can do more within the Department of Defense [DOD] for accountability. My experience in the private sector, especially working for banks, was that they had much more control over what was added to their networks and who could do what than even the Department of Defense does, which was a surprise to me considering how much we think of command and control and leadership within the Department of Defense. Thank you.

Ms. STEFANIK. Thank you.

Dr. Libicki.

Dr. LIBICKI. I believe the administration made a lot of good investment in defensive, in defending networks, and I think that is a trend that should continue. Details, I suppose, we can discuss, but I think the general trend toward putting most of your eggs in the defensive basket is a good one.

In the realm of what I would do different. If you are going to talk up an attack as something that is unacceptable, then you need better attribution, public attribution case, and you need to hit back more strongly. Conversely, if you are not prepared to hit back strongly and you are not prepared to make a good attribution case, maybe you shouldn't make so big a deal of the cyber attack.

Ms. STEFANIK. Dr. Singer.

Dr. SINGER. I echo what was just previously said and add a couple of things. Towards the end of the Obama administration, in the wake of the OPM breach, it put together a series of essentially best practices from the private sector that could be mined for implementation into government. I see those as a key oversight area for Congress and essentially seeing if they are being implemented or not. And, again, I think they are bipartisan in that they are pulling from the private sector.

Similarly, in the very last weeks of the transition, there was a bipartisan commission of experts, cybersecurity experts, that issued a report of what could be done to aid government in this realm. It was lost in the little bit of the conversation. Here too, bipartisan recommendations, implementing those would be a good area.

Finally, the administration created a cybersecurity human resources strategy. This space is not merely about zeros and ones. It is a people problem, and there are all sorts of areas there, and I would look to that and see, is this being implemented or not? It also points to, at least so far in the drafts of the Trump administration's executive orders, human resources hasn't been mentioned. So I would be focusing on that.

In areas of what they can do, what they don't do, there is a wide variety of them that have been mentioned. Whether it is sanctions to—we have done well at pulling in the National Guard as a way of tapping broader societal resource, but that is only limited to what is already in the military.

I would look to the Estonian model or, in essence, the cybersecurity version of the Civil Air Patrol as a way of pulling in broader civilian talent that isn't either able or willing to serve in the military or Guard and Reserves. Ms. STEFANIK. Thank you, Dr. Singer.

So my final more specific question: Mr. Healey, in your written testimony, you discuss how our adversaries are using cyber capabilities as part of a larger strategic and orchestrated influence operations, form of information warfare. The most recent examples are the North Korean hack of Sony, the Russia hack of the DNC, and even 2008, the Chinese hack of both the Obama and McCain campaigns.

In addition to your suggestion to create cyber influence teams with our cyber forces, what more can we do to counter the strategic influence campaigns that are so successfully being waged by Russia, China, North Korea, and Iran?

Mr. HEALEY. Such an important question. Thank you very much. I agree with Dr. Singer on returning to the Active Measures Working Group, which I think is an important step. I think we can start refunding some of those information operations projects that we had done in the 1990s, for example, in [Operation] Allied Force where we had done a lot against Slobodan Milosevic. There had been a lot done in the military professional universities, especially places like National Defense University and the doctrine centers where hopefully some of those people still reside and we might be able to build back some capability quickly.

It also—we obviously need to do this whole-of-government because this clearly isn't a Department of Defense response. It has helped me to think about—you know, we have incidents of national significance to respond to terrorist attacks. We have cyber incidents of national significance, but neither of these fit here. It has helped me to think about an information incident of national significance and think, who would we bring to the table? What agencies would we bring to the table to respond to an information incident of national significance? I am not convinced that we should create such a concept because there is something that strikes me a bit un- American about how we might use that if there is information we didn't like, but it certainly helped me think about how we might improve our interagency response against such actions. Thank you.

Ms. STEFANIK. Thank you, Mr. Healey. I am over my time.

The CHAIRMAN. Mrs. Murphy.

Mrs. MURPHY. Thank you, gentlemen, for being here and for your testimony as well as the Q&A [question and answer].

I represent a district in central Florida that is home to the Nation's largest modeling, simulation, and training industry cluster, which includes a collaboration—which is a collaboration between the military, academia, and industry. The Army command there, known as PEO STRI [Program Executive Office Simulation, Training, and Instrumentation], has been tasked with the cyber training mission for Army.

I was alarmed by a recent study that I saw that talked about the accelerating workforce gap for cybersecurity professionals. This survey projects that we will have a shortfall of 1.8 million cybersecurity professionals in the next 5 years. And to put that in some context, when you talk about workforce gaps in other industries, we are talking in the tens of thousands, but not in the millions. So I found this an astounding shortfall in its size and particularly in a critical area for both national security as well as economic stability.

So I was wondering, you know, you have all talked a little bit about some of the initiatives, workforce initiatives, that could be implemented, but what specific partnerships between academia, government, and the private sector would help to build this talent pipeline in the future, and what role does Congress have in providing investments for and supporting such partnerships?

Dr. SINGER. There is a whole array of activities that can and, frankly, should be undertaken. As was mentioned, there was previously a human resources strategy. It is unclear whether that will be continued or not. I believe it should be in the new administration. If it is not, there should be a similar full-fledged version of it.

Equally, there have been organizations created like, for example, the U.S. Cyber Corps, which is akin to a ROTC [Reserve Officer Training Corps] program, a scholarship program for drawing talent into government. It is unclear what the effect the Federal hiring freeze will have on that. Right now, you have students that are worried that they are not going to be able to meet their scholarship commitments by joining government because the positions won't be open to them.

I would urge Congress and the administration to make clear that cybersecurity is an area that would not be included in that hiring freeze because, frankly, any labor savings that you get will be lost by one breach, one incident.

Similarly, there is a whole series of areas to bring in. As was mentioned, the strength of the United States is in districts like yours and around, so ways of bringing that talent into government for short term. So the examples range from adding a cybersecurity element to the U.S. Digital Service to a program akin to what the Centers for Disease Control has for bringing in talent from the medical field.

Finally, bug bounty programs, which are very cheap ways of incentivizing people outside of government to volunteer to help government. I would urge—the DOD is doing these on a pilot basis. This should be done at every single agency, and Congress can help support that and incentivize that.

Dr. LIBICKI. I mean, there are a lot of programs that have been mentioned, could be mentioned, that could increase the supply of cybersecurity professionals, but if we are talking about the scholarship program, we are talking about hundreds and thousands of people as opposed to millions of folks. And I think thought needs to be given not only to how do you increase the supply but also how you reduce the demand. Let me give you an example.

If you take a look at the Office of Personnel Management, there was a lot of sensitive information, particularly information that you gather as part of doing the security clearance, that was leaked to other countries as a result. Okay. Now, if you just took a cybersecurity perspective, you would say, well, how many people does OPM have to hire in order to make sure that their material doesn't leak?

But there is another way of looking at it. Okay. Do we have to ask people those questions? Do we have to write down the answers? Do we have to put those—digitize the answers that they give? Do we have to make the answers available, and do we have to make the answers available online? And is there some way of finding out where the answers are going online in the circulation?

Okay. None of those things that I describe need a cybersecurity professional. They need ways of understanding how information works. And I think, as a general proposition, there was a tendency to say: We want to compute the way we want to compute. We want no restrictions. This internet stuff is wonderful. We want as much as we can have. But it seems to give us cybersecurity problems. So let's go hire a bunch of cybersecurity folks and sort of spread some cybersecurity on the top.

And if you can't get these folks or you are paying an arm and a leg to get these folks and it still doesn't work because the Russians are very, very talented and the Chinese are very talented, okay, then you might want to consider, how are we actually managing our information? And that leads you to a different place.

The CHAIRMAN. If I could request each of you all, if you would talk directly into the microphone. Sometimes there is a noise outside that is making it hard to hear up here. So thank you.

Mr. Gallagher.

Mr. GALLAGHER. Thank you, Mr. Chairman.

I have a somewhat related question. The Marine Corps Commandant, General Neller, recently stated that using tactical cyber needs to become routine like other technical arms of the service. So when the Arty [artillery] officer shows up or the naval gunfire officer shows up, he needs to be accompanied by a cyber liaison officer.

My concern is that in terms of the cyber talent pool, I don't think a lot of them are enthusiastic about getting a high and tight and joining the Marine Corps. So I am drawn to your idea, Dr. Singer, about something akin to the Estonia Cyber Defense League, but I see a host of practical challenges to implementation, and I think we might have to rethink how we grant security clearances.

Could you just talk a little bit more about that and how we might operationalize and implement such a proposal?

Dr. SINGER. So the approach that Estonia has is a little bit akin to our age-old the minutemen or, more appropriate today, the Civil Air Patrol. The Cyber Defense League there is, it takes people that have been security cleared. So they do go through a clearance process. They are volunteers. They are outside of government. Their talent ranges from people who are hackers to people who are bankers.

So, for example, if you want to understand how to attack or defend a bank, you just don't need computer talent. You need to understand how the systems work. And they essentially volunteer to aid Estonia in everything from red teaming—so attacking voting systems before an election, define vulnerabilities before the bad guys do—to they help with emergency response. It is a little bit akin to the Civil Air Patrol, which gathers people who are interested in aviation, and it ranges from youngsters that are entering the field to people who just want to keep flying, but then they are on call for aviation-related accidents, training exercises, and, importantly, on call at the local, State, and Federal level.

My point is, is that, often in this space, we very appropriately enough say, you know, look, we have got Active Duty, and National Guard has expanded and gotten really good at this, but then we stop and miss the fact that, as you put, there is a great deal of talent that will be forced to be outside of National Guard.

I would also, real quickly, one other point I want to make is that, if we are looking at history, we often talk about the Pearl Harbor parallel, and what General Neller is pointing to is that there are other battles—Kasserine Pass—which were really ones that whether we won or lost was not based on our weapons but our failure to figure out how we command and controlled, how we organized, and that is what I would urge you to be pushing a little bit more on the military side with.

Mr. GALLAGHER. And then, on that point, Mr. Healey, you seem to argue that the reports of a cyber Pearl Harbor have been greatly exaggerated, but I count myself among many Americans who received a notification from OPM after the hack, which some describe as a cyber Pearl Harbor. What is your assessment of the long-term damage caused by that hack?

Mr. HEALEY. Certainly when I thought about my colleagues, my friends who in the future might be negotiating with China over some issue, and I can imagine their Chinese counterparties sitting down in front of them and having their complete SF–86 and the rest of their information in front of them. And I imagine the chilling effect that would have on that negotiation and how America's diplomatic position is going to be significantly worse since then.

But I also take the thought of a devastating attack that leaves thousands of Americans dead. I mean, that, for me, is—it is what we have been thinking about, what we have been imagining that was going to be this catastrophic bolt from the blue, and so certainly that hasn't happened yet. And yet we still, to some degree, allow that to capture our imagination.

So I think we need a little bit more curiosity about what future cyber conflicts might be like and how we respond to those. I think that would put us much better off to deal with the OPMs and to deal with the Russian hacking.

Mr. GALLAGHER. And, finally, Dr. Libicki, among the many terrorist groups that we are fighting kinetically right now, who is the most sophisticated cyber actor?

Dr. LIBICKI. I think you would have to say ISIS. But I think even—ISIS is really good at information operations and propaganda, okay, because in many ways, they say that terrorism is sort of the propaganda of the deed, and so they are integrated within a country—with an organization like ISIS. But in terms of actual cyber capability, there are many criminal groups that are better than all the terrorist groups.

Mr. GALLAGHER. Thank you, Mr. Chairman. I yield the rest of my time.

The CHAIRMAN. Mr. Brown.

Mr. BROWN. Thank you, Mr. Chairman.

I represent a district in Maryland that is perhaps less than 8 miles from Fort Meade, which is home to, you know, several very important agencies and activities in the cyberspace, NSA, Cyber Command, and Defense Information Systems Agency, and we are home to a very large percentage of those high-and-tight cyber warriors. And I know that this committee, over the past several years, has looked at the organization and structure of the cyber force, Cyber Command, as a unified command. We are interested in the dual-hat arrangement between the Director of NSA and as Commander of CYBERCOM, and also we are interested in a strategy for incorporating the Guard and the Reserve.

So my question is—and there are a lot of different activities involved in cyber warfare. At the operational level, do you have any thoughts and opinions on how best to support that combatant commander? We have got cyber mission teams that, my understanding, right now, pretty much operate from CONUS [continental United States], a lot at Fort Meade, some in Atlanta, and pushing those teams out much like the Special Operations Command does, and any other thoughts you have on sort of the operational tactical deployment of these assets.

Mr. HEALEY. Thank you very much, and there are parts of this that remind me of the previous question. You know, the cyber forces, I think, for a very, very long time are going to be high-demand, low-density [HDLD] assets. You know, there is just not going to be enough of them, and in general, when we have got HDLD assets, we try to keep them in a centralized pool so that way—especially keeping them in a place where they can support multiple commands and multiple operations without having to necessarily to deploy to do them.

I think it is going to be a long time before it is as easy to use cyber capabilities as it is to drop a JDAM [Joint Direct Attack Munition] or to send artillery rounds downrange. It is extremely complex, and when you have capabilities, you tend to want to use them sparingly and not in a tactical kind of situation because the adversary will just fix them.

And so the kinds of things that I think have been happening within the Cyber Mission Force have been really excellent, and we hope to see more capabilities and spending in that area.

Dr. LIBICKI. Briefly, I am not too sure I have an answer to your question, but I do have a sense of what it will depend on. First is we need to understand a lot better the efficacy of offensive cyber forces, and the second thing is that we have to understand their depleteability. There is a difference when you surprise somebody in cyberspace, when you pull off something that they weren't expecting, okay. The surprise element tends to deteriorate over time. It is not like an artillery round, which still has the same blast effect for the first as it does for the hundredth.

So that we don't understand a lot, and for these next 5 to 10 years, we are going to have to be playing around with a lot of alternative models until we do have a level of understanding that allows us to make good decisions.

Dr. SINGER. I think your mention of Special Operations Command is an appropriate one. I was actually down there literally yesterday, and it is my sense that that is the likely and I think ideal future evolution of what happens with Cyber Command where it is, as mentioned, it is global in its operation but also can focus down and help in specific commands on a theater level or the like. It also has its own culture, its own approaches to promotions, to different types of budget authorities to reflect kind of its unique role. That is my sense of where Cyber Command can and should evolve to.

Part of that will, as was mentioned, I do think it is time for it to disentangle from the dual-hat leadership structure for both what Jay Healey mentioned, in terms of the intelligence operational side, to just, frankly, it is a human talent. No matter how good the person is, those two roles are incredibly important, and you are getting half their time. They are also very different. To make a sports parallel, it is like having, you know, the coach of the Wizards and the general manager of the Capitals. You know, you wouldn't do that.

The final aspect that I would put in terms of—to aid this in solving a lot of this question is better integration of this into our muddy boots training environments, and when I say "this," I mean both offensive and defensive cyber capabilities as well as the social media side. Our training environment should reflect what the internet looks like now and how we can and our adversaries will use it.

Mr. Brown. Thank you, Mr. Chairman.

The CHAIRMAN. Ms. McSally.

Ms. MCSALLY. Thank you, Mr. Chairman.

Thank you, gentlemen. First, I just have a comment as we are talking about this cyber workforce. Although I agree with you, Dr. Libicki, about managing our information. There is going to be demand. These are going to be jobs that will be out there and growing. And I highlight the University of Arizona South in my district has, you know, taken advantage and seen that coming and really created a cyber operations program partnering with Fort Huachuca, Federal agencies, seeing that this is an opportunity to really train the workforce of the future for government, military, and the private sector, and I think a great example of really how educational institutions need to take advantage of this to provide training and opportunities, you know, for good jobs in the future. So I just want to highlight what is happening at the U of A South.

I am former military. You look at our potential adversaries. They don't want to take us head-on although they are closing some gaps. But we are so heavily reliant on network operations for command and control, for situation awareness, you know, whether that is GPS [Global Positioning System] or how we are managing unmanned aerial systems, even how we are managing air tasking orders and time-sensitive targeting.

If you are the bad guy, you want to go after that asymmetrical potential Achilles' heel. Although we haven't seen it happen, I would like to hear your comments on our vulnerability. Obviously, we are in an unclassified setting, and what we, you know, could do because if we had an adversary go in that direction and try and take us down, we would—you know, we talk about like the AOR [area of responsibility] would go stupid pretty fast, like we wouldn't be able to operate; we wouldn't know how to command and control and give directions to our assets. And I see this as a very deep vulnerability that we have. Do you have any comments on that and what we need to be doing better about it? You want to start, Mr. Healey?

Mr. HEALEY. Thank you. It is tough for me when you ask me the question not to answer first with "Assault Course, Ma'am." So I
would start with—— Ms. MCSALLY. Sorry about that.

Mr. HEALEY. You haven't had——

Ms. MCSALLY. Put him through basic training.

Mr. HEALEY [continuing]. The cyber Pearl Harbor the way that we thought in some way because cyber attacks tend to only take down things made of silicon, things made of ones and zeros, and those are relatively easy to replace.

The more that we are bringing in the Internet of Things [IOT] and the smart grid, the more that those same attacks, instead of just bringing down things made of silicon, can bring down things made of concrete and steel.

Ms. MCSALLY. Right.

Mr. HEALEY. So I am not of those that think cyber attacks have been that bad lately. I really don't, because no one has died yet. I think we are going to look back at these days as the halcyon days when Americans had not yet started dying from these.

So, to me, that is really where I would like to start putting a lot of my time and I think the time from the DOD and from Congress and in trying to see what we can do about—to secure the IOT and keep our adversaries away from them. Thank you.

Ms. MCSALLY. Any other comments from——

Dr. SINGER. I think you are spot-on, and I would point to, you know, so what would make the previous member happy, we spent over $2 billion on construction in the Fort Meade area alone, which is great. We have grown up this capability in Cyber Command, but the Pentagon's own weapons tester found in their words, quote, ''significant vulnerabilities,'' end quote, in every major U.S. weapons program. And that is made up—it has revealed itself in everything from China flying comparable copycat versions of the F–35, which either coincidentally the J–31 looks like it or it is because there were reported three different breaches during the design process, to exploitation during warfare itself.

So, in terms of what Congress can do, I think we need to have a focus on building resilience within the DOD acquisition system. Specifically, establishing metrics and determining where progress has been made or not in our acquisitions process to deal with vulnerabilities in that. So we know they are there; what can we do about it?

I would also add: we can explore how to use Pentagon buying power more effectively outside the defense industrial base. So, for example, entities like Transportation Command have relationships with a lot of different critical infrastructure, how can they incentivize them to get better at their cybersecurity using Pentagon buying power?

Ms. MCSALLY. Dr. Libicki.

Dr. LIBICKI. Three things. First, I think we need a better understanding of our end-to-end vulnerability. Part of the problem in defensive cyber is we tend to chop them up into little pieces and look at the vulnerability of each piece, but in fact, if the bad guys are going to exploit our vulnerabilities, it is going to do it on an end-to-end basis, and this is the basis under which you ought to measure things.

In terms of the vulnerability, as you point out, this is an unclassified session. So my best guess is that heterogeneity and, believe it or not, legacy systems make a big difference because it gives us a lot of ways of doing different things, and I think, in general, the fact that our warfighters tend to be given the authority to do their own innovation is very important because, after a cyber attack, the world is going to look different than it did before, and how do you put the pieces back together becomes very important, and a well-trained military that knows how to think on the spot in different ways becomes very important in the aftermath of a cyber attack, part of the resilience package.

Ms. MCSALLY. Great. Thank you. I had another question about ISIS, but I am out of time. I often—we see ISIS either using the internet to recruit, train, direct, yet the internet was continuing to still work in Raqqa. I have asked many times in this setting, why is the internet still on in

Raqqa? But we don't have time. So we will follow up with you all later. Thank you. I will yield back.

The CHAIRMAN. Mr. Carbajal.

Mr. CARBAJAL. Thank you, Chairman Thornberry and Ranking Member Smith.

Dr. Singer, I am going to build on that but maybe closer to home. An area of major concern is the supply chain vulnerabilities where malicious software, hardware is inadvertently—or exists in the development or acquisition of different systems.

In your testimony, you express concern over the significant vulnerabilities in every major weapons program, extending from breaches of operational systems to original design process. Can each of you speak to how we can tackle these vulnerabilities? What checks and balances can we put in place to avoid developing systems with malicious software or hardware? And what resources do we need to invest in order to protect our supply chain?

Dr. SINGER. So I should clarify this phrase of significant vulnerabilities. That is actually from the Pentagon's own weapons tester. So it is not merely an assertion of mine. It is from our own government's reporting on it. The concern here, again, as you put, is not just merely, what does it do in acquisitions, what does it do in an operational environment like we explored in future scenarios, but it also means it is, I would argue, difficult to impossible to win an arms race if you are paying the research and development for the other side.

And so, in terms of what can be done, I think the question for Congress is where, in using your authority, what are the changes needed in acquisition law, or is it processes, is it policy, to create better requirements for essentially resilience to cybersecurity attack, not preventing it? We will never be able to prevent all of it but build resilience to it.

This also points to the human resources side that we have talked about, and again, this cuts across the board in everything from within the military, as was laid out, to outside and broader society, and it is very exciting to hear—everyone is very proud of the different universities. We need to think about how we can build training for cybersecurity into our education system to create better levels of cyber hygiene. Thank you.

Mr. CARBAJAL. Thank you.

Dr. LIBICKI. There has been a lot of concern about the fact that some of our foreign sourcing leads to vulnerabilities. I am not entirely certain whether we need to do all that much more than we are currently doing. I remember that there was a lot of discussion 20 years ago when people were talking about fixing the Y2K [Year 2000] problem, and there was a lot of handwringing about foreigners working on our code, and therefore, we become much more vulnerable because we couldn't trust the foreigners to work on our code, and I haven't seen any evidence that that really mattered to Y2K or that mattered to vulnerabilities in the immediate aftermath of Y2K.

I think, as a general principle, it gets back to understanding our end-to-end vulnerabilities. Even if a particular product is weak, if there is no way to exploit the weakness, that gives you a certain level of protection. So you do have to look at supply chain vulnerability as part of a broader overall systemic end-to-end vulnerability issue.

Mr. HEALEY. Thank you very much.

I have been impressed with how much has been done on the academic side and within the computer security community on trying to build a trusted system on untrustworthy components. So, for example, if you use end-to-end encryption, like is happening now in Apple, even if you don't trust the systems between you and the person you are talking to, there are tools like end-to-end encryption that can give you much more trust over the system as a whole.

One example in the DOD context is DARPA [Defense Advanced Research Projects Agency] is now putting a system they call HACMS [High-Assurance Cyber Military Systems], the High Assurance Computing Systems—I can't remember the exact acronym—where they are using mathematically provably secure code. They have done this on a helicopter drone. They have given a red team hacker access to part of that drone, and they have not been able to get out, to hack the entire drone and take control of it. So here are areas where you can trust the system even if it has some untrustworthy components.

I would like to also call out what has been happening between the defense industrial base companies themselves. The amount of information sharing, my colleagues tell me, have gotten that, in the past, if the Chinese were to hack one of those companies, they could use that same vulnerability to hack all of them. And it has now been several years where the sharing and the defenses have gotten so good that now they have to use a different software vulnerability on each of these companies. I think that is exactly getting toward the kind of defenses that we need, and it is probably more because of the sharing, which is cheap, than having to add more and give them more money in the contract so they can improve their security.

Thank you.

Mr. CARBAJAL. Thank you for your insight and your wisdom. I yield back.

The CHAIRMAN. Ms. Stefanik, do you have additional questions on your own time?

Ms. STEFANIK. Thank you, Mr. Chairman.

NATO [North Atlantic Treaty Organization] has introduced the Tallinn Manual through its Cyber Defense Center of Excellence in Estonia, which provides an analysis on how existing international law applies to cyberspace. The most recent Tallinn 2.0 Manual focuses on cyber operations and discusses cyber activities that fall below the thresholds of the use of force or armed conflict.

Is this framework helpful in establishing international norms for nation-states, and what, if anything, would you recommend we consider incorporating into U.S. policy?

I will start with Dr. Libicki.

Dr. LIBICKI. I mean, I can say nice things about global rule under international law, but international law is only as good as countries that support international law are willing to support it. In other words, they are willing to put muscle behind violations of international law. And I would—I regard international law as a tool of policy. I do not regard it as a substitute for policy.

At some point, you have to take certain elements of international law seriously enough to say, "This is unacceptable, and this is what we are going to do about that," and this is in turn part of a broader discussion, which I urge that we have, about what in fact constitutes thresholds. Okay.

Part of the problem with using international law as a base, as was obvious in the Tallinn 1 Manual, is that there is a lot of disagreement among people about what in fact constitutes legal behavior, and you don't have the same judicial mechanism in the United States where you can point to the opinions that are rendered by judges to say, okay, there is a consensus that this is a way it is and this isn't the way it is. We don't have that. Okay.

So, in the end, international law has to be supported by nation- states—by countries and their willingness to take risks in support of law before it becomes actionable.

Ms. STEFANIK. Thank you.

Mr. Healey and Dr. Singer, do you have anything to add?

Mr. HEALEY. I am a huge fan because it takes a lot of the arguments off the table. You know, instead of arguing, well, arguing from scratch if we think something is an act of war, not now; we at least have a place to come from. And that helps a lot. Now we can argue what part to do about it. That is really what has been tripping us up, I think, more than anything, is not what to call something or what thresholds to set, but what are the actual policy tools and how are we going to use them in each instance, and hopefully now we can focus on that.

Ms. STEFANIK. Dr. Singer.

Dr. SINGER. I am a huge supporter of it as well. I would just add two things to it. The first is to recognize that there is not just this process but a broader webwork of agreements and norm building that is going on in everything from bilaterals with allies to multilaterals, be it at NATO to all the way up to United Nations. And I think a key area for action for Congress is to essentially request of the administration, what is your overall strategy here, how does this all fit together, and, most importantly, are you not going to let this fall by the wayside, because it is clearly advantageous to the United States to shape these norms in a way that restores global cybersecurity.

The second most important thing is to recognize that the quickest way to undermine norms and laws is to take an action when they are broken, and we have seen repeated instances, specifically by Russia, in everything from attacks on power grids that were no-go areas, such as in Ukraine, to most recently this broader campaign that I mentioned. And so, if we want to norm build, we also have to take actions besides just write things down in treaties.

Ms. STEFANIK. Thank you.

In some of your testimonies, you have talked about our increasing capabilities when it comes to attribution. My question is, how good are we at doing battle damage assessment [BDA] in cyberspace? Are there areas or capabilities that we need to invest in to improve our ability to do BDA?

Mr. HEALEY. Do you mean against our—when the attack is against us or—— Ms. STEFANIK. Yes.

Mr. HEALEY. Yes. Here, I think a lot of work that has been happening in the Information Sharing and Analysis Centers as well as the new policy from the past administration for Information Sharing and Analysis Centers to try and come together and get that coordination done within the affected sectors themselves or the affected companies, that depends so much on which sector has been hit to try and figure out the level of disruption.

Some, like finance, are extremely good at this. Their regulatory agencies are banging on the door to find out what happened. Other parts of our critical infrastructure, like water, aren't going to be as strong, and that underlines, I think, how good the sector organizations are, how well they are regulated, for example, rather than anything specific to determining the level of disruption and the damage.

Ms. STEFANIK. Dr. Singer.

Dr. SINGER. This is one of those key areas, I think, to delve deeper into in the muddy boots training side. So, for example, if you lose 10 percent of communications, it is only if you actually go out and exercise it that you understand that maybe it doesn't have a 10 percent compromise on you; maybe it actually means your entire organization can't work. Or, similarly, if it is not you lose access but that you can't trust communication. If one time the adversary inserts false information, be it into GPS or false information into an order, does that mean that you no longer trust the system itself, so the entire system goes down?

So that is one of the areas where I think we need to evolve it more and do our own training to understand the effects of it. That is the only way. Ms. STEFANIK. Thank you. My time is expired.

The CHAIRMAN. Ms. Rosen.

Ms. ROSEN. Thank you, and I really appreciate all of you being here today. Thank you, Mr. Chairman.

My question is about the disentangling of the NSA and Cyber Command. And so I see some of the benefits and challenges. I would like you to expand on that a little bit and especially about how that relates to our ability to respond dynamically to threats or challenges as you see them and our ability to be fast and flexible there.

Mr. HEALEY. Thank you very much, Congresswoman Rosen.

The most dynamic part of America's cyber defenses is not Fort Meade, and it will never be at the Pentagon. It just isn't. They can't—pretty much no part of the U.S. Government is actually creating and maintaining cyberspace. One of my colleagues that used to—a former Army major that then went on to work at Verizon— said, look, if there is an attack, we at Verizon and our colleagues and our companies, we can bend cyberspace if we need to; we can change the physics of the space to blunt this attack in a way that is incredibly difficult for places like Fort Meade and U.S. Cyber Command to do. U.S. Cyber Command simply just doesn't have the levers to be able to respond agilely enough to attacks against us.

They can certainly attack back, but they are not—they are not tied in in the same way as these companies are. And so, because I believe that the private sector is the supported command, they have agility, they have the subject-matter expertise, and they can bend cyberspace if they need to, that our money is best spent, rather than trying to recreate that at Fort Meade, find ways to help make sure what they can do better.

Dr. LIBICKI. You have asked an interesting question, which, unfortunately, I don't have a clear answer for because I am still thinking through it. Okay? But a lot of what you do with Cyber Command, vis-a-vis NSA, depends on what you actually want Cyber Command to do. If you are thinking of what Cyber Command does as part of a broader information operations area, then you need to bring Cyber Command in with other parts of the Department of Defense that deal with information operations. And this is not a—this is not something that is currently on the table.

Ms. ROSEN. Cyber Command, doesn't it also execute?

Dr. LIBICKI. Right.

Ms. ROSEN. Right.

Dr. LIBICKI. In terms of its—in terms of its offense mission is what I am referring to. Okay? In terms of its defense mission, it is a coordination between Cyber Command and the way the networks are currently managed that becomes an important component. And for a long time, NSA has had that responsibility to improve the security management of DOD networks.

If you are looking for Cyber Command to think in terms of a general analysis of the vulnerability of other people's militaries, then you may want to bring them in together with other folks who look at the vulnerabilities of other people's militaries that are not necessarily digital zero and ones but, in fact, arise from the interaction of the various components of their militaries. And that is about as far as I have gotten in my thinking, unfortunately.

Dr. SINGER. So I think we have laid out earlier some of the rationales for it, and it ranges from the split, as you note, between, essentially, the evolution of the missions from intelligence to Cyber Command becoming more and more operational, both offense and defense, having training requirements and the like. As I mentioned, there is the double-hat problem of just human talent.

There is another aspect of this that I think is interesting to talk with you about is go back to the original rationale for why they were double-hatted. It was both because the creation of Cyber Command, it didn't have its own culture, didn't have its own human talent, but it also was because there was a concern that the head of Cyber Command would not be able to speak with a voice or authority that would get Congress' attention.

Ms. ROSEN. Right.

Dr. SINGER. Post-Snowden, the absolute opposite happened where you are more interested— maybe not you individually, but Congress is more interested in the NSA surveillance encryption debate side. And we even saw that in the confirmation hearings for the head of Cyber Command.

So I think for this wide variety of reasons, it makes sense to split them, but I would not do it instantaneously. I would do it like the transition that we had with the Joint Forces Command where the mandate, so to speak, of the last commander was figure out how to disentangle this in a way that doesn't compromise effectiveness.

Ms. ROSEN. Thank you.

Well, as a former computer programmer and systems analyst, I have about a million more questions about the public-private partnership versus privacy. We don't have the time to do it today. I hope you will come back, and I will be able to ask them all. Thank you.

The CHAIRMAN. You can use the gentlelady as a resource as you go on ahead. That is what is clear to me. Mr. Scott.

Mr. SCOTT. Thank you, Mr. Chairman.

Gentlemen, many of my questions have been answered, but I want to go back and focus on a couple of things. The Y2K issue was approximately 20 years ago. It was not intentional, but my question has always been, as we talk about malware and digital and Xs and Os, one of the vulnerabilities that we don't talk about much, which has been mentioned before, has been the supply chains and the ability to perhaps embed things in hardware prior to the manufacturing of the actual equipment.

I go back to just, for example, the GPS system that we put in an airplane or a radio system that we put in an airplane, could it be preprogrammed to stop working at a certain point in time, in which case that would give your, certainly, major adversaries, your near-peer adversaries, a distinct advantage over you, and that if they knew that you were going to lose radio communications at a certain point in time, that would obviously be an opportune time for them to go on the offense.

And so it seems to me that we have this constant testing, if you will, of capabilities among select few countries. When one of those countries finds a weakness, the question is how far do they go in exploiting it, I guess, before a cold war actually becomes what we would acknowledge as a true war.

I listened to your comments on the split of leadership at NSA, certainly interested in further discussion on that. But I would like for you to speak, if you would, towards the future.

Dr. Healey, you said that we don't have the levers that the private sector has to bend cyberspace, I think is the way you put it.

We obviously have Active Duty personnel. We have National Guard personnel. National Guard has had a tremendous amount of success in helping us. What is the—what does the Cyber Mission Force look like 20 years from now? What are the decisions that have to be made to make sure that we have that cyber force?

Mr. HEALEY. Thank you very much. It is a great question. And to put some context, I am not taking swipes at Cyber Command. I was one of the initial cadre of what became Cyber Command. When I was a young captain in the late 1990s, I helped the headquarters there set up what was to become the Joint Task Force- Computer Network Defense and was one of the 21st—one of the first 25 cadre members there, and then it went on to grow to be U.S. Cyber Command.

When I think about—it is a great question and what that force might look like. One of the futures that I start thinking, and I am saying, what would happen if we went down that—if—what cyber conflict might look like in 10 years.

Last year, at—DARPA funded a contest called the Cyber Grand Challenge in which they had different supercomputers discovering their own vulnerabilities and throwing—discovering vulnerabilities and attacking the other supercomputers on stage, which then had to run through their programming and come up with automated defenses. And, certainly, when I am thinking about what cyber conflict might look like in 20 years or 10 years, that to me seems like somewhere obvious to start in where DARPA is already thinking.

So just imagine how—what that might mean for the Cyber Mission Force where we have over 6,000 people at Fort Meade, and other places now, preparing for a fight. Well, if the future conflict is going to be malicious software that has got a back end over a supercomputer telling it what to target next, how to change to avoid defenses, you now need your own supercomputer to try and defend against that. And I think that has just tremendous challenges for military doctrine, for organizations, and certainly, for staffing.

Mr. SCOTT. That brings me to another question. I mean, obviously, a lot of these people, they are extremely intelligent. We need to have the ability to work with these people. They may not be interested in joining the military. They may not work, certainly, full- time or part-time. I mean, for lack of better terminology, I mean, do we, when we see this problem coming, deputize a cyber posse like the old days where you bring people in that you have never worked with before?

And, Dr. Singer, I know—interested in your opinions.

Dr. SINGER. That is why I am an advocate of, look, there is great talent within Active Duty. National Guard has been a way to pull in. We have reorganized, so we can pull in that talent, you know, that already has cyber skill sets. But at the end of the day, as you note, there will be a wide range of people who either are unwilling to serve in the National Guard and Reserves or they simply won't qualify for physical reasons, whatnot. And so we need to create alternative pathways to draw people in beyond just contracting them.

And that is why I am an advocate of both this Civil Air Patrol cybersecurity equivalent to expansions of the U.S. Digital Service to include cybersecurity, simply looking at outside of this field, what are like models that we know work? How do we use those to bring in cyber talent?

And then, lastly, I would point to the bug bounty program. The— you asked, you know, what will this look like? The people that participated in the Pentagon's first bug bounty ranged from off-duty government workers to people working in business doing it nights. My favorite example was an 18-year-old who did it in the middle of their AP [Advanced Placement] test, who volunteered to help defend Pentagon networks and reportedly he did it because he just wanted the T-shirt. So we have to have a means of pulling in all this wide variety of talent. That is what makes America great.

Mr. SCOTT. But you also have to get them cleared from a security standpoint. You have to have them operate under some agency out there, and those are things that, I think, need—we need to have that outlined before the attack happens.

Dr. SINGER. Absolutely.

Mr. SCOTT. Mr. Chairman, I apologize for going over.

The CHAIRMAN. That is fine. Interesting discussion. Mr. O'Halleran.

Mr. O'HALLERAN. Thank you, Mr. Chairman.

I guess I want to go back a little bit to Mr. Scott's issue, because I have a concern that what we are doing here is without deterrence, without clearly showing deterrence that we are in this never-ending spiral of more and more people, more conflict between budget for cyberspace and the budget for defense; how do we pay for it, that the people that are attacking us are spending far less to attack us than we are to stop the attacks. And so it appears that the deterrence factor has to be something that is credible, as Mr. Libicki said.

I am just trying to understand how we start to slow down that cycle. It is a great full-time employment issue for a lot of young people that are coming out of our universities, but it is a serious question as far as our long-term capability to be able to defend ourselves without trying to deal with the deterrent side in a meaningful way—if we do not deal with it in a meaningful way.

So how does that all occur? And, Mr. Libicki, I would like to start with you.

Dr. LIBICKI. I think, ultimately, the way you discourage people from attacking you is to give yourself an architecture, the relationship between information and systems, that reduces their value— what they get from attacking you in the first place.

And even if we had an effective national deterrence policy, we would still have many other threats from criminals, from insiders. And so one of the advantages of defense and resiliency is that defends against people, no matter what their motivation and no matter what way we can and cannot reach out and touch them.

Mr. O'HALLERAN. And I take it from your comment that you don't feel we are at that point yet where we have the system that can deter like that?

Dr. LIBICKI. I think we have made a great deal of progress. I think we have a lot more progress to make. It is going to be a long challenge.

Mr. O'HALLERAN. Dr. Singer.

Dr. SINGER. So there are different forms of deterrence. And because of the Cold War experience, we typically focus on the idea of deterrence by overwhelming retaliation.

There are many things for the people in Fort Meade to be upset with Mr. Snowden about, but the one thing he did reveal is that there is no question of our offensive capability. And yet, as we see, the attacks continue. So it is not like the Cold War where there is mutuality here and that, you know, someone attacks us and we respond in a like manner. So if we are thinking about retaliation, it is going to be better using those other tools of American power to influence actors that have both attacked us but also others looking to it. And that is why I am very pointed about the Russian campaign and our lack of a response to it has incentivized a wider array of actors.

Secondly, there is a different form of deterrence which wasn't possible in the Cold War called deterrence by denial or it's resilience. It is the idea that I don't attack you not because you are going to hit me back, but because my attack is not going to succeed. You will shrug it off. And importantly, resilience would be a useful building activity. Whatever the form or type of attacker, you build good resilience, it is good against criminal actors, state actors, you name it.

And in my written testimony, there are a whole series of actions that we can take to raise our resilience levels and therefore make attacks against us less successful and, therefore, less likely.

Mr. O'HALLERAN. Thank you.

And, Mr. Healey, just to go a little bit further on this. We just talked about Russia during the Cold War. It got to the point where they just appeared to not be able to afford to continue on with the path.

In this instance, we have a situation where those that are attacking us can afford to keep going because our cost ratio is much higher than their cost ratio. How—just how do we start to stop that? I understand what Dr. Singer just said, but, again, the architecture is just not there right now, and our cost is just exploding.

Mr. HEALEY. There are new architectures and new things that are coming down in the computer field that I think will help. We have been doing a New York cyber task force at Columbia University to say what can we make a more defensible cyberspace, a more defensible America, more defensible sectors, more defensible companies. And so, for example, going to the cloud. I was astounded how many of the bank chief information security officers and others that were saying absolutely allows you a more secure foundation to build that from the ground up. The CIO [chief information officer] thinks he is going to do it for cost reasons, but really you do it for security.

I would also like to add, I tend to be very hesitant when it comes to trying to raise the adversaries' costs more directly, but I certainly think when it comes to Russia, we have got a national mission team. They are looking into red space, able to disrupt the Russian influence operations and cyber attacks. I think, absolutely, we should start thinking about that to help out France, German elections as they are coming up. Thank you.

Mr. O'HALLERAN. Thank you, Mr. Chairman.

The CHAIRMAN. Thank you. Mr. Wittman.

Mr. WITTMAN. Thank you, Mr. Chairman.

I appreciate our panelists for joining us today. Dr. Libicki, I want to start with you. You have spoken very much about building an offensive capability. I have a particular interest in that, because I think it is the way that we can make our adversaries use their resources to defend their systems. I think that is extraordinarily important.

Give me your perspective about how in the realm that we see ourselves in, especially with the United States Navy with new systems, unmanned platforms, and what we have to do to create command and control there, how do we not only protect those systems, but how do we look at vulnerabilities that our adversaries might have with their systems so that their time is taken up not in going after our links within our systems or looking for weak points there, but what they have to do to defend their systems. And how do we most aggressively pursue that?

Dr. LIBICKI. Well, there are a number of standard ways for exploring other people's systems. And one of the best ways is actually buy a copy of them and then run it in our test labs. We did that throughout the Cold War, and I don't think our activity has slowed down very much.

To the extent that they use international components in their systems, they already have a certain amount of familiarity with that. We probably pick up a great deal of electronic intelligence just by listening to these components communicate with them over the air. Okay? But let me actually address your question by asking a question, for which I am not quite too sure there is a good answer, but I will do this anyway.

To what extent do we want to tell folks or hint to folks that we have an ability to interrupt their information systems? Okay? On the one hand, it gives us a great—a certain amount of deterrence. It reminds people who are doing a lot of—throwing a lot of stones that they live in glass houses, and it reveals our intention to go after their glass houses, which I think is very important.

On the other hand, you want to do it in such a way that it doesn't look overly aggressive, aggressive but not overly aggressive, and you want to do it in such a way that it doesn't give away too much of how we actually do our business.

So there is a lot of trade-off to be had here. I think we are in a good position where we are given credit for a lot of capability without necessarily having to show it. I don't know what the depletion rate of that confidence is. Okay? But right now I think it is pretty high.

So we have American defense officials, certainly in the last administration, I think in this administration, who have hinted from time to time that we have a great deal of capability, and they need to watch themselves, but to maintain that confidence, or lack of confidence, in their mind, I think is a challenging problem but not an insurmountable one.

Mr. WITTMAN. The next question. How do we, as we look at where the future brings us with educating and training our military members and leaders today for the challenges they will face tomorrow within the cyber realm—and I have been an advocate to say all the way from the basic training level, tactical level, all the way up to the strategic level, there needs to be a common theme of training and educating everybody in the military as to the cyber sphere that they are going to operate in.

Give me your perspective on where you see things currently going, maybe even some of the efforts that are undergoing through your experience that are happening maybe at places like the academies, and what needs to happen there to make sure we, from top to bottom in our fighting force, emphasize the cyber realm as much as we do the kinetic realm?

Dr. LIBICKI. I am glad you asked that question, because it allows me to speak on behalf of my employer. I think the Naval Academy does a really good job on this. We have two semesters of requirements for all naval and Marine Corps officers; one they take in their first year, one they take in their third year. I have a little experience with them, because I teach a lot of freshman this sort of stuff. We also have a cyber operations major. This year, we will be graduating about 40 folks. And one of the nice things I like about the program is that we spend years two and three on the technical education, and then starting a bit in year three and into year four, we give them the policy perspective.

One of the biggest shortfalls in the area of cyber is you have a lot of technical people that can't talk policy; you have a lot of policy people who don't have a rich enough foundation in the technology. And I believe the Naval Academy is graduating officers that, in fact, have a background in both of them. And I think that is very beneficial, and I think it is something that I—speaking ex cathedra that I think the other two military academies also should take a serious look at.

Mr. WITTMAN. Are there any efforts underway currently as far as facilities or things that might be there in the future to make sure that we are even enhancing that experience with things like, you know, a secure facility like a SCIF [sensitive compartmented information facility] for them to be able to learn and operate within?

Dr. LIBICKI. Well, as you happen to ask, we are building a cyber building, the Hopper—Hopper Hall, I think it is called, on campus. It should be ready in about 2019, and it is supposed to have a SCIF.

Mr. WITTMAN. Very good.

Thank you, Mr. Chairman. With that, I yield back.

The CHAIRMAN. Mr. Veasey.

Mr. VEASEY. Thank you, Mr. Chairman.

I want to ask Mr. Healey a question. In your testimony, you recommended that the U.S. needs to take further steps to deal with foreign influence in cyber realm. And I wanted to ask you if you could elaborate more on what those steps look like and which agency you would have spearhead those?

Mr. HEALEY. Yes. Thank you, Congressman Veasey. I think it is a tough question, because one reason why I think we have turned to the Department of Defense to help us out on cyber issues, has been they were there with the capability when they were needed.

Many people have been very disappointed that it has taken the Department of Homeland Security so long to get themselves up when it comes to dealing with cyber issues, and yet DOD has been there quietly providing capabilities for a long time. I see the same problems are going to affect us here when we are talking about influence operations. DOD clearly should not be in the lead on such things, but we could easily imagine ways that the Department of Defense can bring their amazing capability to bear on this. They have already been studying information operations. I think they should be coming to Congress with different projects to fund within the—probably within the cyber branches, for example, 24th Air Force or 10th Fleet, to start rebuilding that information operations capability.

And also, blowing—blowing on the coals of where those—that information operations capability resides, particularly National Defense University. And, hopefully, that can kick off, while the interagency process is figuring out how better to deal with this. I think there obviously will be a role for Justice and for State and the Department of Homeland Security, but it is going to take them much longer, I think, to get their capability up to speed, unfortunately.

Mr. VEASEY. Thank you very much.

And, also, I wanted to ask about just the relationship between the private sector and the government moving forward when addressing these cybersecurity concerns. You know, there have been, obviously, lots of talk about the government being able to have a back door to be able to go into some of these devices so they can go back and find out exactly what was taking place. But then, also, there are other—there are apps and things like that that are overseas that these—that the companies here in America don't necessarily have the same access to that wouldn't be able to unlock some of those clues that we may be seeking in case of some sort of a terrorist attack. So I just wondered if you had any thoughts on that at all, either—any of you.

Dr. SINGER. So across the board, if you did a poll—and, actually, they have been done—of cybersecurity experts, consistently they would say that building in back doors is the best way to create greater vulnerability for the wider public and the Defense Department systems themselves that we have talked about. So that is why you find very few advocates of that within the community. And, oh, by the way, people would just move to other systems.

So the challenge, I think, you know, to move—that is a known known. The challenge between the public and private sector relationship now, one of the key areas is just who does the private sector turn to for help when there is an incident?

The administration towards the—the Obama administration in its last year began to clarify that a bit, but it is not yet enough, it is not yet clarified. And in my sense, among the proposals that I have got there is, you know, the idea you need a one-stop shop, a key place for them to go.

I wanted to circle back, though, to your prior question about influence operations. Much of this, the activity to counter it, is going to have to happen outside of the Defense Department. It is everything that we mentioned from the creation of an Active Measures Working Group to debunk lies and make it harder for people to spread them. It is to the debate over critical infrastructure and our election systems has, I believe, wrongly focused just on voting machines when, clearly, the targets are political organizations.

They should be having the same kind of information sharing that competing banks do, and same kind of linkups to government. The activities during the 2016 election would have been stopped if just the FBI and the DNC had had a better means of communication and had been able to trust each other.

To—again, there are other elements to this. On the intelligence community side, Congress should be requesting briefings on just what these influence operations in the broader spread of social media means for the likelihood of conflict itself, how it is affecting popular sentiment among adversary states and the like.

Mr. VEASEY. Thank you very much. Mr. Chairman, I yield back.

The CHAIRMAN. Thank you.

Mr. Bacon.

Mr. BACON. Thank you, Mr. Chairman. I stepped out to get a couple of votes in, but good to be back.

My question is about the dual-hat relationship between Cyber [Command] and National Security Agency. We heard some testimony today that suggests there is a good thing to break that into two different [inaudible] for staffs. [Inaudible] I was at Fort Meade earlier this week, and there are indications to do the same, but I see warning signs of that. Right now, the expression of cyber teams, there seems to be a cohesion of, you know, a synergy between the NSA side and the—some of it, sometimes it is one person, goes to title 50 to title 10 back to title 50. Eventually, at some point, you are going to get different priorities, different visions, and I see where it can break down that synergy that you need and that cohesion.

What are the benefits of moving away from a dual-hat relationship and getting two different four-stars? And isn't there a better way to elevate Cyber Command than going down the path that some are suggesting? And I would just open it up to anybody that would care to answer.

Dr. LIBICKI. Let me make sort of a tactical—a tactical statement here. We tend to think of attack and espionage as two different things. Right? Attack is your title 10 thing, espionage is title 50. We shouldn't have the same people doing attack as we have doing espionage. But in practice, the two may be a lot more similar than we think.

Let me give you a scenario. Let us say that I can attack a network, inject messages in a network and tell the bad guys to meet at a particular place. I get there an hour before they do, tactical engagement, I win. Right?

Mr. BACON. Right.

Dr. LIBICKI. Scenario two. I listen until I find out that they are going to meet in a particular place. I find out where, when. I get there an hour before they do. The tactical results, fairly similar. Right? Why do you want one organization doing one and one organization doing the other because we happen to have defined injection as a title 10 issue and interception as a title 50 issue?

I think what those folks are doing—and sort of as a broader issue, a lot of what you can do with interception of information these days has a lot more tactical relevance than it did 20, 40, 60 years ago. If I can get into your equivalent of Blue Force Tracker and just listen, the tactical advantages I would have would be tremendous.

Mr. BACON. So you are positing here that you should have a totally separate Cyber Command that has that reconnaissance capability? Is that what I am hearing?

Dr. LIBICKI. Well, if you end up with that reconnaissance capability, you have now recreated a large chunk of NSA.

Mr. BACON. That is right. So wouldn't you want a single-hat or a dual-hat four-star?

Dr. LIBICKI. Well, that is a different voice, and again, have to give more thinking about. You certainly want some very strong XOs [executive officers] in both of them. Right?

Mr. BACON. Right. Two different——

Dr. LIBICKI. So that, in fact, the XOs are running the agency.

Mr. BACON. Which is what we have today.

Dr. LIBICKI. Which is what we have today, so it depends on the quality of the XO.

Mr. BACON. Mr. Healey, it looks like you have a different thought.

Mr. HEALEY. I think both Peter and I were looking to jump in.

One, I don't mind creating a friction. I think this is the most escalatory kind of conflict we have ever come across. I don't mind having some brakes on that, just like we don't mind brakes on using nuclear capability.

The people that say let's keep them together, they want to optimize offense, intel, and defense, and it is true, keeping them together does optimize that. I want to optimize America's overall defense, and that means optimizing the integration with the private sector.

Look at what we have done. We have folded information assurance directorate farther into the signals intelligence directorate at NSA. I would have loved the option to keep that out so that they are able to better work with America's private sector, which I think are the ones that are truly doing the defense.

Of course, it makes sense to optimize those things. I just think we—there is a higher priority when it comes to this.

Mr. BACON. Mr.—Dr. Singer.

Dr. SINGER. I think there are two points here. The first is, just because you divide the dual-hat structure doesn't mean that they can't continue to work effectively together. And we can look at models outside this space for how you have seen task forces and interagency teams and everything from, you know, General McChrystal, what he creates, to engaging into counter—counterinsurgency efforts in Iraq, which brings together talent from across services, other agencies, to how we approach counterdrug efforts down in SOUTHCOM [Southern Command].

So just because you split them doesn't mean you can't operate in this interagency manner. And, frankly, as Jay puts it, it may be easier to bring in other elements either legally or because of their willingness to work with.

And then the second is, I would echo Jay's point, there is a worry, you know, but what if they might disagree? That is a good thing. That is a good—that is our system, and disagreements then allow the next tier of leaders—it airs ideas and then allows the next tier of leaders to get both perspectives. So I would say the friction between them isn't necessarily 100 percent bad, and in a lot of situations, it might be good.

Mr. BACON. Okay. Well, I appreciate your inputs. I just see a warning—I have commanded five times, and I have seen a good rapport, and I have seen some where there wasn't that good a rapport. And I could see two different four-stars with different visions, and folks that would pay for it would be those 133 teams that have to be working well together. So thank you. I yield back, sir.

The CHAIRMAN. Mr. Courtney.

Mr. COURTNEY. Thank you, Mr. Chairman, and for organizing this hearing, which is a big one for this committee.

First of all, Dr. Libicki, I just wanted to, you know, add a footnote to your comments about the academies. I represent New London, Connecticut, where the Coast Guard Academy, and they are moving very swiftly over the last three or so years to boost their cyber curriculum. And I mean, they are, you know, very, very much focused on that and doing good work. So I am sure, you know, the Naval Academy has obviously been leading the way, but I just wanted to at least add that sort of little extra comment there.

And I really have just sort of one question. One of the members talked about back doors. And you may have already covered this, and I apologize, because I was in another committee. But, I mean, we are seeing, you know, obviously, a lot of programs flow through this committee, large platforms whether it's long-range strike bomber, F–35, *Columbia* class. And, you know, the model for building these platforms now relies on a pretty extensive supply chain, which can be, you know, firms and companies that are, I mean, tiny. And I just sort of wonder if you had any comment about, you know, how we sort of address that issue? I mean, it is a big one in terms of just, again, the number of actors that participate in, you know, pretty sensitive projects.

Dr. SINGER. Sir, you are exactly right. There is a series of potential vulnerabilities, and they extend, again, across from the software-based attacks on the design process, i.e., you know, learning how to model, to copy it all the way to operational side, and then the same thing when you think about the hardware, the potential of hardware hacks on the chips themselves. And the result is that it is—it can play out in anything from lost future arms races or future sales to foreign markets to actual loss in battle.

The thing is that the Pentagon senior leadership, I believe, is aware of this problem, but the answer to it has been kind of uneven in its implementation. And I would urge the committee, essentially, to, you know—you are the ones who best know, whether it is through a hearing or a report. We need to figure out, when it comes to these kind of vulnerabilities, how in our acquisition system can we build up resilience, and is it law changes that need to happen in that buying process or is it policy changes that need to happen to incentivize resilience across the supply chain.

And to echo something I said earlier, we shouldn't just think about this, though, in the defense industrial base. DOD has a lot of buying power to other parts of the economy. Where can it use that influence to aid cybersecurity writ large for the Nation?

Mr. HEALEY. And if I may, like many cybersecurity problems, this comes down to who pays in many cases. If you are talking about Lockheed Martin having the defenses to keep out Chinese attackers, well, we can say, all right, Lockheed, you have to pay for that. But for many of the companies that we are talking about here, buying in a more secure way for the supply chain is going to be more expensive, and we can't always expect them to foot the bill on that to choose a more expensive part for where there is a little bit more trust. And, of course, when it comes down to more pay, then it is going to be services and committees like these that are going to have to help decide that.

Dr. LIBICKI. I would like to make a statement. We mentioned back doors, but I think front doors are also a problem. Okay? Imagine you have a very capable—a very great capability, a very sensitive capability. And you say, I want these people to be able to access it, and you are happy. And then somebody from the outside— not the outside, you know, somebody who is part of your group, or whatever, part of the military, says, oh, I also want an ability to access it. Okay. Well, we give you access. And I also want the ability to access it. Sooner or later, you end up trying to figure out who has got the ability to access it. How many more people do I have to protect? How many more people do I have to monitor? Because there is a tendency in this world to just expand accessibility because it can help people do their jobs. And every time you expand accessibility, you expand the attack surface. And if you are not careful, every time you expand the attack surface, you have created another route for somebody else who doesn't have your interests at heart to go in and try to play with your system. So a lot of cybersecurity means saying no to people.

Mr. COURTNEY. I yield back.

The CHAIRMAN. Chairman Conaway.

Mr. CONAWAY. Thank you. The officer corps is being trained at the academies, but this exact same training is going on for enlisted ranks at Goodfellow Air Force Base in San Angelo, Texas. Give a shout out.

A lot of speculation in the media or in this world about how soon it will be before robotic soldiers take the place of the fight in the kinetic world. How soon will AI supplant the need for— and, Mr. Healey, you mentioned a bit of computer—computers fighting computers. But how quickly will AI supplant the need for all these human beings to be able to defend these networks and do what we do?

Mr. HEALEY. I will take it quickly, and then yield to Peter, since he kind of wrote the books on this.

One, because I was an alumni at San Angelo, I think it is probably going to come more quickly than we think, as many of these developments do. The part of it that worries me the most—and by that I mean 10 years. The part of it that particularly worries me the most is that on the defensive side, many people are thinking that artificial intelligence, new heuristics, better analytics, and automation are going to help the defense. That if only we can roll these things out faster, that we will be better and the system will be more stable.

I think that these technologies are going to aid the offense much more than it aids the defense. Because to defend against these kinds of attacks, you need your own supercomputer. That is fine for the Department of Defense. We have got them lying around.

But for America's critical infrastructure, they are not going to be able to afford such defenses in many cases. Certainly, small and medium-size enterprises and mom and pops are not going to be able to. And so that is why that future, in particular, worries me if it goes down that direction, because it leaves much of America undefended.

Mr. CONAWAY. Let me ask one other thing, and you can comment on either one of these. But most of these cyber warriors, the human versions, will be in protected enclaves, probably here in the continental United States, where most of the work will never need, really, to be able to field dress an M–4. However, there are others in this group that may be fully deployed again and protect the enclaves, but they should have some familiarity with it.

Is the DOD doing a good job of being able to split out those guys, who are going to be in an enclave forever, don't need to look like a soldier. They probably don't act like one, and they don't take orders like one. But is the Department looking at, in terms of the near term, need for human beings, this group of folks that really don't look good in uniform and don't need to know how to fight other than with a keyboard and—or versus AI I think that I mentioned earlier?

Dr. SINGER. So on your first question on AI, I point to, as an example, at recent hacker convention, DARPA competition had AI competing to bug hunt, and it was won by one from Carnegie Mellon called MAYHEM, and it was able to take on a task that human hackers, bug hunters, it would take them a long period of time, and did it quite quickly.

So the point I would make here is that much like, you know, you mentioned robotics and drones and conventional warfare, we have a couple of kind of disruptions potentially coming in the cyber conflict side. AI would be one, another would be quantum, where when I say disruption, it is not just when is it going to happen, but we don't yet know is it going to privilege the offense or defense, what are going to be the effects of it.

So in my written testimony, I advocate that you should hold a classified hearing on trying to find out where do we stand in these technologies versus likely adversaries, because they are critical. We don't want to fall behind on them.

On your question of people, the answer, to be blunt, is no. We have done a very good job of organizing existing talent within the military, be it an Active Duty or starting to retool the National Guard, but we don't have a means for pulling in people outside the military who are willing to serve but not to formally join or unable to because of some requirement. And that is why in the written testimony I propose a sort of series of actions and organizations that could help us do that better.

Mr. CONAWAY. Dr. Libicki.

Dr. LIBICKI. I just want to add one thing. It is important to get talent into the technical side of hacking and counter-hacking, but from a military perspective, it is also important to have people who understand how offensive and defensive cyber warfare fits into all of the other elements of warfare so they can be presented in an integrated manner. And for that, I don't think you have much of an alternative but a militarily trained individual, whether an officer or enlisted.

Mr. CONAWAY. Clearly, it is not either/or. It is both. Because the physical requirements to run a keyboard and a mouse pad are dramatically different than somebody who has got to even go downrange and run a keyboard.

I appreciate your perspective, and I yield back.

The CHAIRMAN. I would just note an editorial comment on the AI discussion. It seems to me that we are always a lot better at developing technologies than we are the policies on how to use them, and that certainly seems the case there.

I would like to back up and maybe rehash a little bit some of the topics that you all have touched on.

Starting with the role of the military to defend the country in cyberspace. If there were a bunch of bombers coming toward refineries in the Houston ship channel, we know what we would expect the U.S. military to do to defend that private infrastructure. If packets were coming through the internet against the same refineries, under the Obama administration, if it caused death or significant economic damage, I guess, not really defined, then the military could get involved to defend that private infrastructure. You have got to make judgment calls, all this is happening at the speed of light, et cetera.

So I would just appreciate reflections from each of you on the appropriate role of the military in defending nonmilitary—in defending the country, private infrastructure especially.

Dr. LIBICKI. I think there are a lot of things that the military can do, but I think it is also—there are a lot of things the military cannot do, and a lot of the difference, by the way, between the two is the sort of a technical difference. Let me give you an example. Let us say we lived in a world where the technology of firewalls was good enough, and the economies of scales of firewalls were such that it made sense to have a national firewall. Right? You could say, well, that could be a role for the Department of Defense. It could be a role for another part of the Federal Government, et cetera. Let's say the Department of Defense, because it often takes classified information to make a firewall run well. Right? And if it turns out that that was a large part of the solution, there would be a strong argument for the military.

But the state of firewall technology does not suggest a ground for that sort of optimism. There are—it doesn't defend against zero- days. It doesn't defend against built-in malware. It doesn't defend against encrypted stuff. And by the time you sort of do a positive and a negative, you end up saying, I don't think the firewall is going to get us there, and, therefore, I don't think whatever role is associated with running the firewall is going to get us there either.

I don't think it is a question of, well, physical is going to be military and cyber is not going to be military, because there is a sort of existential difference between the two. I think it is a matter of what tools do you use and then how do you deploy those tools. And if the tools that you need to use, for instance, have a lot to do with architecture, have a lot to do with systems administration, have a lot to do with training, then the role for the Federal Government is correspondingly smaller.

If, however, you are depending on barriers, if you are depending on classified intelligence, then the role of the military is larger. And it might be, for instance, that 20 years from now, with the technology, that the role of the military is much larger than it is today because the tools are different. It is entirely possible that 20 years from now, the role would be smaller, because we are looking at a different set of tools entirely. Okay?

It is not an ideological ipso facto issue. You have to follow the technology in order to think about roles and missions.

The CHAIRMAN. Interesting. I want you all's perspective too. In addition, you have got to figure out who is doing it. Because if it is the most sophisticated sort of state actors, then it is pretty hard for anybody, other than our military, to defend against it. But I would be interested in you all's perspective on this.

Dr. SINGER. So I think it is interesting to use your example to look back at history. So we have the obvious, a bomber plane crosses into our territory, drops a bomb, military responsibility. But we had a real—fortunately, that never happened in World War II or ever. But we did have a real-world example in World War II where German submarines dropped off saboteurs, and the Navy was responsible for hunting down the German submarines. In the midst of an all-out national conflict, it was the FBI that was in charge of the saboteur hunting down.

So I point to—you know, we have wrestled with these before in the physical domain. So I think when it comes to the questions of roles and responsibilities, the way we have divided out so far for the military makes a great deal of sense. It is very clear offensive action should be governmental, should be military responsibility.

I would note, there's been a push recently for, hey, shouldn't the private sector be able to hit back on its own. I would argue that is a very bad idea. It is a bad idea for the same reason that vigilantism in general is a bad idea. Makes you feel good about yourself, it doesn't actually do anything about the effect. When you move into politics, if we have got private actors out there hitting foreign entities, they might think it is a U.S. state action.

So that is clearly military. Defend its own networks, again, clearly military, pulling in aid from the private sector. Where it gets questionable is in this what should the military do to aid the private sector.

And as I think Jay noted and probably will note, it is not just a question of what kind of roles and responsibilities. There is also the hard reality that the private sector knows its own systems better. So it is going to be the one best equipped to defend itself, set aside all of the other kind of appropriate questions.

So, for me, the parallel here is just like when there is a natural disaster or some other thing, the military should be on call to aid.

When it moves into a situation of war, where it is an act of violence, political in nature, now we have moved into there is a clear role for the military. So they should be able to aid if they are called upon by other agencies, but if we are short of an act of war, I don't want them fiddling around with power grid networks or the like.

The CHAIRMAN. Okay. And, Mr. Healey, as you answer, I just want to add another layer here. So according to press reports, a foreign actor destroyed computers owned by Saudi Aramco. Is that destruction of property that justifies this kind of added layer of military involvement if something like that were to happen here?

Mr. HEALEY. Without a doubt. I used to be the vice chairman of a group called the Financial Services Information Sharing and Analysis Center [FS–ISAC] that coordinates response and information within the finance sector. And there is a bunch of military help that I could have used, but it is not generally the military help that we think. I would have loved to have had just some senior NCOs [noncommissioned officers] or good junior officers that knew how to respond to incidents and could keep their head so that when we had a bad incident, that they could help us get ready for the response and what was going to happen next.

I could easily imagine a situation where attacks against the finance sector, where we have to call for fires, where we have—the banks have to say, we are not going to be able to open for business tomorrow unless we get this taken care of. How are we going to do that, that call for fires? The private sector is the supported command. We need to start thinking about this.

On the finance sector, is finally starting to push an issue of how do we get our intelligence requirements listened to? We are the ones that are on the front line. How can we have some communication with the intel community just like any other customer?

To me, this is so difficult, because the attacks have largely been so inconsequential, not causing death and destruction. So I like to step back and say, well, imagine if we are not in a gray area. Imagine it is black and white. People have—Americans have just died because of foreign cyber attack. In the Aramco case, large-scale attacks against our refineries. What do the American people, what does the American President now looking to, to the military? It is not support to civil authorities. We are going to be looking for that military to step up.

And the last thing I will mention is, in historical analogy, during the Battle of Britain, they invented something called the Dowding System, where they were having to track what incoming fighters, what is the radar telling us, which fighters are we going to divert. And so I see us needing a modern version of this Dowding System that includes the private sector. So that when you have these kinds of attacks, we have got information that is coming in and we can figure out how to handle those defenses.

I don't believe that is probably going to be at the NCCIC [National Cybersecurity and Communications Integration Center], at DHS where it is right now, and it might not even be at Cyber Command. We might need a more American model that brings together a better partnership.

The CHAIRMAN. One other thing that occurs to me as you were talking is, we are going to— if that is the case, we are going to have to have a government decision-making ability in appropriate time. You cannot take every one of these cases to the NSC [National Security Council] and deliberate on it for a month. Maybe we are moving more in that direction, but it has obviously been a problem before.

Let me yield to the distinguished ranking member of the Emerging Threats Subcommittee, Mr. Langevin.

Mr. LANGEVIN. Thank you, Mr. Chairman. I want to thank you for convening this panel. It has been a great discussion. I wish I had been here for all of it. I was at a Homeland Security briefing on cybersecurity, on this topic as well. So—but I appreciate all of the contributions you all have made in various aspects to this dialogue and the work you are doing in this field.

Dr. Libicki, let me start with you. What metrics do you believe we should have in place to determine if cyber operations, both offensive and defensive, are effective or not?

Dr. LIBICKI. Well, that is a very interesting question, because metrics are one of the hardest things in security. Right? The problem with a lot of defense is if the other side is only interested in stealing your information, and you don't know about it, you think you are in good shape, when, in fact, you are not in good shape.

One of the things that our intelligence community and our law enforcement community has gotten some traction on is trying to figure out, by looking at the other side, what people have stolen from our own side in terms of—in terms of how good our defense is. In terms of our offense, that—some of it you can do directly. If you maintain a presence on the other person's network and you want to attack it in a certain way, as long as that attack doesn't kick you out of that network, you have a fairly good platform for how you see the other side react.

But, in general, I think when you are judging offense, you have to take a look back and say, what is the broader overall military effect that we want to have and how do we measure that particular effect, not merely the cyber effect? I think there is often a tendency—particularly because cyberspace operations are so technical— to measure the quality of cyberspace operations and did we move the ones and zeros without measuring the bigger picture, did it help us win the battle/campaign/war?

Mr. LANGEVIN. Anybody else?

Dr. SINGER. I would add in a couple of other elements. When you are thinking about on the offensive side, we have typically framed it in terms of classic military operations where, clearly, many, if not most, of our adversaries are looking at them through the lens of influence operations. So it is not how many websites did I take down or your access to GPS or the like, but it is how did I shape the overall environment? How did I, to put it bluntly, hack your hearts and minds? And that is something that we need to pay attention to both in adversary hands and ours.

The second is on the defensive side. When we are looking for metrics, again, they are not just sort of the obvious ones of detecting attacks. What we are seeing in the corporate sector moving more to this resilience strategy is—a key is recovery time. So how long after I have detected— how long after I have been knocked down do I get back up quickly? And this points to, again, the concept of deterrence by denial. If you have got good recovery time, then you have nullified what the attacker did to you.

Mr. LANGEVIN. Thank you. Yes, it is one of the things I am wrestling with right now is, you know, how do we assess metrics. And we have the NIST [National Institute of Standards and Technology] standards, for example, which are important, but, you know, the degree to which they are being adopted and if they are being adopted, is the framework effective? We don't have any sufficient metrics right now to measure that.

So let me ask, while I have—so I have a little bit of time left, to all of our witnesses. In your opinion, what are the greatest policy challenges that the Department is facing with respect to military operations in the cyber domain?

Dr. LIBICKI. I would say that the greatest challenge the DOD faces is understanding its own vulnerability and understanding its own vulnerability on an end-to-end basis.

Mr. HEALEY. I think that is a fine answer. I am still—I struggle when I talk to DOD officers and officials, and they seem pretty uncurious about how tomorrow's cyber conflict might look different than yesterday's. They are so deep down into looking at the ones and the zeros and talking about network speed and hazy borders that I would love their challenge to pull out. I mean, we are so busy doing the destroyer engagements, we are not thinking about fleet actions or what actually winning is going to mean in this field.

Dr. SINGER. I would echo the concept here, again, of while it is almost natural and in terms of identity and thinking to focus on the offensive, on the how do I use this, how do I take it to the enemy, the reality is that resilience is the side, that building up DOD resilience would give us a greater advantage. It is just, to put it bluntly, not as sexy, and it is not something that has the same appeal.

The second to add to this would be multidomain operations, understanding how fires from one domain might affect another domain. And a key element of this is recognizing that a lot of what we are talking about is not just cybersecurity but moves into the space of electronic warfare [EW] where adversaries, in particular Russia, have been making deep, deep investment in that. And as they showed off in Ukraine, particularly in the ground forces side, they are probably better than us.

And this is an area where, again, we may need to think about, you know, coming off of decades-plus of counterinsurgency, have we shrunk too much our electronic warfare capability, not just building out cybersecurity capability, but do we need to build up EW side too?

Mr. LANGEVIN. Thank you all very much.

The CHAIRMAN. Mr. Khanna.

Mr. KHANNA. Thank you, Mr. Chairman, for convening this panel and for your leadership of our committee.

My question is for Mr. Healey. I was very pleased to read in your testimony that the center of U.S. cyber power is in Silicon Valley and not in Fort Meade. Of course, I represent that area, and that is what the many folks in the Valley think.

My question for you concerns coordination. The reality is, today, we have many private companies that have their own basic cybersecurity defense, and we would never have that each company have their own private military. Is there a way to have information sharing or a platform between these companies? Is there a way to have information sharing between them and the government in a way that doesn't compromise classified information?

Mr. HEALEY. It is a great question, and I am very happy that I had a chance to come back and add some details to these remarks.

Some of those already exist and are relatively well funded. We can still build capability. Others don't exist, and we hope that they will stand up. Others are in place but relatively starved of resources.

I have been, as I mentioned, the vice chairman of the FS–ISAC. And we only shared information and coordinated response for people that paid to be members; largely, that meant Wall Street. We got about a $2 million grant from Treasury to re-up our technology, but we had to include all 13,000-plus financial institutions in the United States. And now the FS–ISAC is winning awards for being the best information-sharing and response organization. I think that is the best $2 million that we spent in U.S. Government on cyber ever.

Compare that. DHS right now is spending millions of dollars a year on a vulnerability database that is in trouble right now. One of my colleagues was running an open source version of that that had something like four times as many vulnerabilities in it for $10,000 a year, and they ended up having to close up shop because they were starved of resources. So there is so much that is happening out there, and we don't necessarily have to recreate that within the Department or within the government, because it already exists.

Others that I will mention—and I am sorry, I won't break out the acronyms in the interest of time. NANOG [North American Network Operators Group] is an operating group that helps coordinate the main network service providers. NSP–SEC [Network Service Provider–Security] does the same and was critical in the response to the denial of service attacks on Estonia. And there are many of these groups out there that are already helping. And I think with some small targeted grants like the FS–ISAC could, we are talking about a few million dollars, they might be able to build a secretariat, they might be able to include new technology, and I think really make a difference. You saw this with the defense industrial base sharing where just saying, go ahead, you can share, and you won't get an anti—in anticompetitive trouble led to significant differences.

Mr. KHANNA. I would love to follow up with you offline and get your thoughts on this. But if you were to prioritize, then, one or two things that we on the committee could do, what would those be in terms of the funding?

Mr. HEALEY. In this area? The first thing I would want to do, and this is this committee but also maybe Homeland Security, is have the executive branch go through each of several different kinds of the main incidents that we faced—botnet takedown; denial of service attack; major malware spread, like Conficker; counter- APT [advanced persistent threat]—and go through in a disciplined way, who took what actions, who took what decisions based on what information, and what happened next.

I think if we went through that process in a disciplined way— include decision modelers in that. I mean, again, we are talking about a few million dollars. And you come out with that and now you know the actual decision makers, you know what the information sharing requirements are. We can build our cyber incident response plan around that, and then we can help use grants, if necessary, to start building the capability where it is needed to make sure that is going to happen better next time. Thank you.

Mr. KHANNA. Thank you. Well, thank you for your testimony, and I hope we can work with you on these issues.

Thank you, Mr. Chairman.

The CHAIRMAN. Thank you. I want to go back to resilience for just a second. Now, you all talked a lot about it. Obviously, the drive for the Department of Defense—and you have all mentioned, you know, an Internet of Things; everything is connected; every platform is a sensor— so to increase your capability. And yet, as we think about the Russian hacking, one of the reasons people had confidence in our voting system is because every State was different, and so that diversity, the fact that they were not all linked together, was part of the resilience that made it much harder for any actual changes to happen in the voting.

So how do you balance that? You want to be more effective. We don't have enough money, and yet does not this drive to have everything connected reduce our resilience?

Dr. SINGER. There are a couple of things to note. I mean, we should be clear that—well, I will put it this way. Part of how you find that optimal mix of—what you are laying out is essentially kind of both diversity but new and old, and the constant story again, whether it is your personal cybersecurity or DOD cybersecurity is this battle between convenience, effectiveness, and security, and that is the same—so you find that optimal space, frankly, by doing, by training, by testing.

I would use the example of the election side, though, to illustrate this. There has been testing done that shows, yes, voting machines are vulnerable. It is not that the diversity kept us safe. It is that, in the 2016, the threat actor didn't go after them. The threat actor went after not the voting machines but the voting public, and this is again a lesson to the DOD side, is it is not always about how does my system work; it is about the humans behind them, be it their hearts and minds and sentiments or their awareness or the like.

So, you know, we shouldn't tell ourselves that we have been made secure because an actor didn't go after something. The actor went after something else and was effective at it and, now, again, are going after other allies. They are not targeting, as far as we are aware, the French voting machines or the German voting machines. They are targeting the voting public and getting potentially maybe more out of it.

Mr. HEALEY. And I think it is a great point, and I really want to associate myself with Dr. Singer's point in this and your previous question, because to me, when I hear the military talking about cyber and the third offset, I get really, really worried because it seems, from a lot of my colleagues that I hear from, they are thinking that that means more offense and offense is going to be how we can use cyber as part of the third offset to move in a way that our ally—that our adversaries can't.

I think you have hit exactly on resilience is the way that we can do that. Having better cybersecurity so that we can have deterrence by denial and they are not going to be able to affect us is a critical part of that. I have been very heartened to see what has been happening in the military the few years where they are saying, "Let's operate—let's unleash the red teams and exercise this so that they can really show us what they can do and really affect the exercise," whereas, normally, you would not let them affect the exercise goal.

Just like the Air Force used to make sure pilots could operate through jamming, they are now starting to say, what can we do when we don't have the internet? I think that kind of resilience is really where we are going to have the third offset.

The CHAIRMAN. I agree completely on exercising when your networks go down or something; that is true. And I just mention among the hearings we are planning in the future is one that looks more broadly at, however you want to describe it, hybrid warfare, attempts to influence policy short of traditional methods of warfare. Certainly what the Russians are doing are some examples. Chinese are using their economic power. Others—I mean, this is one of our key challenges, I think, which you all have touched on, but we don't have time to get in.

Thank you all for being here. It has been very helpful. The hearing stands adjourned.

[Whereupon, at 12:08 p.m., the committee was adjourned.]

APPENDIX

MARCH 1, 2017

PREPARED STATEMENTS SUBMITTED FOR THE RECORD

MARCH 1, 2017

Prepared Testimony and Statement for the Record of

P.W. Singer
Strategist at New America

At the

Hearing on "Cyber Warfare in the 21st Century: Threats, Challenges, and Opportunities"

Before the House Armed Services Committee

March 1, 2017

Cyber-Deterrence And The Goal of Resilience:
30 New Actions That Congress Can Take To Improve U.S. Cybersecurity

Hackers working on behalf of the Russian government have attacked a wide variety of American citizens and institutions. They include political targets of both parties, like the Democratic National Committee, and also the Republican National Committee, as well as prominent Democrat and Republican leaders, civil society groups like various American universities and academic research programs. These attacks started years back, but have continued after the 2016 election. They have hit clearly government sites, like the Pentagon's email system, as well as clearly private networks, like US banks.

In addition to attacking this range of public and private American targets, over an extended period of time, this Russian campaign has also been reported as targeting a wide variety of American allies. These include government, military and civilian targets in the United Kingdom, Czech, and Norway, as well as now trying to influence upcoming elections in Germany, France and Netherlands. Overall, reports are that Russian cyber attacks on NATO targets are up 60%, against EU institutions up 20%, in the last year.

This is not the kind of "cyber war" often envisioned, with power grids going down in fiery "cyber Pearl Harbors." Instead, it is a competition more akin to the Cold War's pre-digital battles that crossed influence and subversion operations with espionage. Just as then, there is a new need for new approaches to deterrence, that must reflect a dual goal to defend the nation, as well as keep an ongoing conflict from escalating into physical damage and destruction.

While Vladimir Putin has denied the existence of this campaign, its activities have been identified by groups that include all the different agencies in the US intelligence community, the FBI, as well as multiple allied intelligence agencies, who have seen the very same Russian efforts hit their nations and various international organizations (most notably the World Anti-Doping Agency). This campaign has also been established by the marketplace; five different well-regarded cybersecurity firms (Crowdstrike, Mandiant, Fidelis, ThreatConnect and Secureworks) have identified it. This diversity of firms is notable, as such businesses are competitors and incentivized instead to debunk each other's work. Indeed, even the most prominent individuals, who first denied the existence of the hacks and then the role of the Russian government in them, now acknowledge this campaign;

this now includes even the US president ("As far as hacking, I think it was Russia." President Trump stated at his January press conference).

It is time to move past the debate that consumed us for the last year. The issue at hand is not whether Russia conducted a series of cyberattacks on the United States and its allies. Nor is cybersecurity a concern for only one political party. The real question now is whether and how should the United States respond?

A Wider Strategy for a Larger Problem

Russia's attacks are the most notable events in cybersecurity, but they are only one aspect of a larger threat landscape. In cyberspace, the malevolent actors range from criminals stealing personal information or holding ransom valuable corporate data (though, here too there is a major Russian role, with over 75% of ransomware coming from Russian-speaking parts of the online criminal underground; and Russian criminal groups have repeatedly been used as an enabler for the Putin state) to governments like China, which have been accused of breaking into government databases like the OPM in a cyber version of traditional espionage, as well as largescale intellectual property theft.

Just like in the real world, in this online landscape, though, we must weight threats. And here too, the scale and power that states can bring to bear far outweighs that of non-state actors. For example, while "cyber-terrorism" and the activities of so-called "Cyber Caliphate" of ISIL sympathizers have garnered great media attention, their most noted exploits so far are mostly annoyances like hacking a US military command's Twitter feed and posting pictures of a goat. By contrast, no single threat actor has brought malicious cyber activity together in the wide-ranging and brazen manner in which Russia has done, targeting not just individuals and organizations across our society, but the fabric of democracy itself.

So what can be done to defend America in this realm? The following is a strategy that, reflecting the nonpartisan nature of this realm, is able to be implemented with support from leaders of both parties.

1) Restore Deterrence

Cyberweapons have proven their value in espionage, sabotage, and conflict. And the digital domain will be as crucial to warfare in the 21st century as operations on land, air, and sea. Indeed, the cyber front of any war between the United States and China would feature not just military units like Cyber Command or the PLA's Unit 61398, but also non-state actors that might range from Chinese university cyber militias to Anonymous hackers joining in the fight with their own goals and modes, much as what has happened in the online ISIS battles.

This is a good illustration of another misperception: Cyberweapons are increasingly useful tools of espionage and war, but they are not akin to "weapons of mass destruction." The fear of a single big thermonuclear tit for tat maintained the nuclear balance; indeed, treating nuclear weapons as no different from conventional weapons is what many feared would unravel MAD. Offensive cyber capabilities, by contrast, are a key part of the toolkit to be used in both hot and cold conflicts. Indeed, the US has already crossed this line by openly admitting to conducting offensive cyber operations against ISIS.

Reflecting this dynamic, we should continue to build our offensive cyber capabilities and the deep investment we have made at organizations like Cyber Command. A key element to maintaining superiority will be to *invest deeply in game-changing technology breakthroughs in this space, most notably AI and quantum, to ensure a US lead is maintained. As such, congress should request classified briefings to assess where the US stands in this space in relationship to likely adversaries.*

As we move forward, though, we must recognize that, just as in the past, technology is not enough. The key to effectiveness will be in doctrine building and integration; i.e. how we meld technologies and activities in the cyber domain with conventional operations in the air, sea, land, and space. Indeed, if there is a historic parallel to worry about in a future conflict, it is not merely Pearl Harbor, but a digital version of the 1942 Battle of Kasserine Pass, where a US military failure to bring together technologies and units across domains helped contribute to the early losses of World War II. This points to how the time has come to *establish Cyber Command's long-term status and disentangle the "dual hat" leadership structure with the National Security Agency.* These two valuable organizations work in the same realm, but they must reflect different organizational culture, goals, and processes. Of note, among the original rationale for this "dual" structure was concern that the leadership of Cyber Command would not have enough stature with Congress; instead, the post-Snowden debates have meant that Congress has more often become interested in their NSA role.

Building deterrence, however, is not merely about military capability. We must have a unified strategy that cuts across agencies and is willing to understand and use all the tools of power and policy, not just those that encompass the zeroes and ones of software or malware. In these, we should seek to leverage our strengths against others' weaknesses.

The Obama administration moves in late December to sanction Russia for targeting US democracy are a good start, albeit too little and too late, <u>criticism that the congressional leadership</u> was quick and correct to make. It is thus equally correct for the legislative branch to back these words with action, *by turning the sanctions against Russia for its 2016 elections interference into law and strengthening them further.* This will make it harder for any moves by the Executive Branch to set them aside (as both <u>White House aides have noted in press conferences</u> and Mr. Trump has hinted would be the case at his press conferences). Instead, strengthened sanctions would show Mr. Putin that the nation of Truman, Eisenhower, and Reagan is still willing to stand up to Moscow, rather than <u>shower it with praise</u>.

Deterrence is not about punishment for punishment's sake, though, but seeking to find pressure points to influence future actions, both by that actor and others looking to its example. Here the overall weakness of the Russian economy and its oligarchic structure are choice leverage points (indeed, it is sad that the US is being bullied about by the <u>13th largest economy in the world</u>). In thinking through targeting for cyber deterrence, we can sometimes see what regimes fear most by what they try to ban discussion of. This points to a particular focus to expand: *targeting financial assets of Mr. Putin and his allies, especially those held outside the country in real estate and tax shelters,* even those with US and Western business partners. Sanctions, especially tying up oligarch money/visas, to Russian cyber interferences are valuable in two ways. The first is to shift malicious cyber activity from being low cost-high gain to the attacker, changing Russia's calculus, as well as a signal to future attackers. IE, we should want it 'on-the-record' that this kind of action crosses the line and warrants retaliation, which would also be useful for a rapidly forming body of international law and norms that are in flux.

Outing these assets should also be the target of any covert cyber action (the Russian regime's outsized anger at the publication of the Panama Papers, showing where just a small portion of its money was hidden around the world, reveals an area to exploit further). The same twin goal of outing and defanging networks should also be placed on enablers of the attacks, focusing on *revealing to the wider community the digital and financial infrastructure that has been used to conduct the attacks themselves*, which would reduce their utility for future attacks.

The point is that, unlike in the Cold War, there is no need to hit back within the limited time window of the other side's missiles in flight. Cyber deterrence building can come after the fact of an attack and in other realms. The defender can go after the structure used in the attack, other assets valued by the attacker in other realms, or even those assets valued by third party actors that have influence on the attacker. Thus, the response to a cyber attack can range from hitting back with a like cyber attack to alternative pathways like sanctioning companies benefiting from stolen fruit to personal level actions like threatening to revoke valued visas or business deals for regime leader or oligarch family members, etc. Indictments of individuals involved in hacking might also serve a purpose not of actual prosecution and punishment, but as a different means of surfacing data about attribution, or to make access to the global financial system more difficult. The goal is a wide dynamism that complicates attackers' calculation that they will make any clear gains.

So too must our deterrence building goal align with the building of global norms, through activities that range from international treaty negotiation to the use of sanctions.

This leads to a fundamental change from the typical discussion of deterrence. In the Cold War, everything was targeted, from military bases to cities full of civilians, but outright attacks crossed the line. Today, the situation is inverted. While unwanted, some cyberattacks will have to be allowed, while certain targets must be made anathema.

Not all 'cyberattacks' are formal acts of war. No one wants their state secrets stolen, for example, but it is part of the expected dance of great powers in competition. Hence while the theft of secrets from the OPM was a clear loss to US security, it was not an attack that was beyond the pale. As former NSA and CIA directors have explained, the breach at the OPM was more a "shame on us" than "shame on them" situation. By contrast, there are other cyber attacks that may not be clear acts of traditional war, but they should be a focus on norm building to prohibit. For instance, introducing the digital equivalent of a dormant Tasmanian devil into a nuclear power facility's operating system or other major civilian infrastructure should be off limits to both sides, not merely because it would be disproportional if actually used, but because simply the act of deploying it risks accident or even interpretation as an incredibly escalatory step of preparing for war.

Continuing to set and reinforce these guardrails has to be one of the key activities in the various bilateral and multilateral efforts that the US government makes in this space on norm and law building. These extend from the webwork of agreements on cybersecurity that we are building with our allies to the two U.N. General Assembly resolutions that call for respect of the laws of war in cyberspace, to the Tallinn Manual process. In order to ensure this track is not abandoned in the upcoming administration, *the Congress should hold hearings on what US norm-building strategy in global cybersecurity will be moving forward, with a special focus on actions that can be taken to support the Tallinn Manual 2.0.*

Yet, for all the laudable work in building norms, what threatens to undermine any guidance of behavior is inaction when acts clearly violate the norms. One of the consistently agreed upon norms across global and US discussions is not to target clear civilian infrastructure with the intent to cause widespread damage (as opposed to a goal of monitoring or stealing information), even more so outside of a context of a declared war. Such attacks are viewed as violating the norms of necessity and proportionality that underpin the internationally agreed upon laws of war.

Yet, in December of 2015, this line was clearly crossed in an attack on the Ukrainian power grid. More than 230,000 civilians lost power, in what has been positively identified as a cyber attack by both local authorities and international experts, and US officials have identified Russia as the attacker. It was the first proven takedown of a power grid, the long discussed nightmare scenario. Yet, in the story of action and consequence that is the key to maintaining norms, we had clear action, but as yet no clear consequence. Just as with the attacks on our political system, a pattern of not responding builds a different kind of norm and incentive. *The Congress should hold hearings on what US strategy is in response to this new realm of attack, both in how we plan to aid Ukraine and foreign partners from suffering such attacks in the future and how we plan to better defend the US system*, to ensure this act is not swept under the table.

2) Build Resilience

This strategy to influence attackers should be joined with an effort to build our own resilience to their influence. "Resilience" is the ability to power through an attack and shake it off, thereby limiting the gains to the attacker and recovering rapidly from any losses. It is also known as "deterrence by denial." The idea here is, by making attacks less beneficial to the attacker, you make them less likely. Most importantly to the problem that we face in the diversity of cyber threats, it is useful for responding to them all. The great value of building resilience is that it applies not just to Russia, but to any kind of cyber attacker and any kind of cyber attack.

Unfortunately, despite the attention, rhetoric, and money the United States government spends on cybersecurity, it is still far from resilient against cyber attack. For every gain, there is still a major gap to be closed. In the military, the construction budget alone for Fort Meade, the combined headquarters of the NSA and Cyber Command, reached $2 billion by the end of 2016, and the force will add another 4,000 personnel. Yet, the Pentagon's own tester still found "significant vulnerabilities" in nearly every major weapons program, that extended from breaches of operational systems all the way back to the original design process. The multiple reported breaches of the F-35 program and the "interesting" similarities between the next US strike fighter and its Chinese twin the J-31 is an example of changed dynamics: It will be hard for the US to win any arms race if we are paying the research and development cost for the other side.

The Pentagon leadership is aware of these vulnerabilities, but the overall implementation of resilience measures is still uneven, especially within the DoD and federal government acquisitions process. *A focus on building resilience, establishing metrics, and determining where progress towards them is not being met, should be a key oversight priority for Congress.* Among the measures needed is to *determine where if any, changes are needed in either law or Pentagon buying processes to bolster resilience to cyberattack.*

In the broader federal government, the cybersecurity budget for 2016 was 35 percent higher than it was just two years ago. Yet half of security professionals in these agencies think cybersecurity did not improve over that same period. The reasons range from continued failure to follow basic measures – the requirement for personal identification verification cards dates back to 2004 but still is not fully implemented -- to a failure to take seriously the long-term nature of the threats we face, most importantly in a world of renewed geopolitical competition. The exemplar of these failures was the OPM, which dealt with some of the most sensitive government information, and yet outsourced IT work to contractors in China -- despite warnings going back to 2009.

There have been various drafts of new Trump administration Executive Orders on floating about online, so it is preliminary to comment on them, other than to say that they seem focused on initiating a series of evaluations and reviews. For the new team to further study the problem and how we are organized is perfectly sensible; but it is well past time that we begin to act on areas where there is general agreement across political lines.

One of the lesser noticed studies of the last administration was to identify a series of best practices that the top firms in private industry use in cybersecurity that could be brought into government, as well as create a bipartisan commission of experts, which issued its own set of recommendations during the transition period of Dec. 2016. These range from identifying high-value assets that need to be better protected and recruiting top human talent to accelerating the deployment of detection systems. *Ensuring the implementation of these measures to raise federal agency cybersecurity could be one of the most important things that the new Congress could do to limit our insecurity in cybersecurity.* And the fact that they originate from market lessons and bipartisan advice should make them politically doable for leaders of both parties. *The Congress should request of the new administration a yearly report on its progress on meeting these metrics, and use them to identify any key funding or programmatic gaps.*

As information systems ubiquitously underlie key governing functions, states and localities are increasingly critical to the nation's cybersecurity. Investing in robust relations between the federal government and state and local actors is essential to (cyber)securing the nation. Recognizing the essential role played by non-federal government actors on the 'front lines', *the Congress should identify where the federal government can better coordinate with and aid local authorities. This includes efforts to clarify the respective roles of and responsibilities for federal and state entities, as well as disseminating the many existing and helpful resources to state and local actors, who are currently operating in relatively resource-starved environments.*

This same uneven implementation plays out across industry. While corporate boards are now talking far more about the problem, cybersecurity spending as a portion of IT budgets is still roughly a quarter of the rate within government IT budgets, while only 25% of key industry players, for example, participated last year in Information Sharing and Analysis Centers (ISACs), which share needed cyber threat data -- the same percentage as in 2014. The outcome is that some sectors, like banking, take cybersecurity seriously, while others, like health care, manufacturing, and infrastructure, remain behind the curve. Of note to the concerns over Ukraine power grid attack is that despite this real demonstration of the risks, experts worry that US companies have not implemented key steps to better protect themselves, not just against the tactics used in December, but how they will naturally evolve in the future. *Congressional action is needed to establish whether critical infrastructure firms, most especially in the power sector, actually have implemented needed measures.*

This concern extends down to the personal level. Unlike in the Cold War, individuals both face personalized cyber threats, but also can contribute more to national security. During the Cold War, "duck and cover" was about all that a population could do when it came to nuclear deterrence. Today, the vast majority of Americans use the Internet, and they can actually make a difference in its defense. Whether we are talking about career civil servant or a citizen trying to secure sensitive information, the human is an incredibly important part of the system of defense, if not the most important. Over 90% of cyber attacks would be stopped by basic measures of cyber hygiene, from two factor authentication on accounts to using different passwords for their bank accounts and fantasy football teams. *Increased congressional support for cyber hygiene efforts, including in our schools, would be a valuable aid to national security.* Just as we should seek the latest technology, a truly robust government approach would include the latest innovations from behavioral science to improve cybersecurity. Reflecting this, *Congress should also include support for programs that support social and behavioral science insights to improve cybersecurity policy outcomes, specifically in the creation and improvement of cyber hygiene-related policies to boost adoption.*

How this all ties together into one strategy is that we have to rethink the role that government can play in linking cybersecurity policy, markets, and citizenry behavior. In other words, government can and should play the role it plays in cybersecurity that it does in other realms, from health to transportation.

Sometimes government can be a trusted provider of useful information to both business and the wider public. And sometimes it can go further to help shape individual and market incentives. For instance, the government created Center for Disease Control (CDC) to fill key gaps in fighting disease, funding research on under-studied diseases, and serving as a trusted exchange for information provided by groups ranging from universities to drug companies. *The creation of an equivalent cyber CDC could meet some of the same needs in cybersecurity.* This track will also build upon how the question in cybersecurity is no longer the debate of public sector vs private sector response, but rather which part of the public sector should companies turn to for what aid? The last administration's PPD41 started this clarification, but there is more required; it should not be for the private sector to have to navigate which part of the government to call in each circumstance.

Similarly, U.S. buildings are filled with "EXIT" signs and fire extinguishers, while cars have seatbelts and crash bags. These demonstrate the efficacy of government in creating *both* voluntary standards and actual regulations to increase security. These regulations are then bolstered by insurance laws and markets that use the combined power of the public and private sector to incentivize good behavior and best practices. Such a system has positively shaped everything from building construction to driving habits.

So too, the government should support not merely research on the basic standards of Internet security , like the laudable NIST process, but now work to backstop them with the nascent cybersecurity insurance market. Like many other new insurance markets, cyber-insurance certainly has a long way to go and key questions to figure out, but we can't let its growing pains now keep us from reaching for a system that would make our industry, as well as citizens, consumers and the entire nation, more secure. If Congress can aid in spurring that market to further develop, it can potentially have a massively positive effect on national security.

Last year, the cybersecurity marketplace collected $1.6 billion in premiums. It sounds like much, but is a drop in the bucket compared to the overall scale of the insurance industry (which collected over a trillion dollars comparatively), the scale of our digital economy, and the scale of cybersecurity risk at both a personal, business, and national security level. Less than half of the Fortune 500 have insurance protecting them against cyber incidents (and, in turn, incentivizing and guiding them to undertake best practices to avoid and mitigate these risks), while among mid-sized firms, some 18,000 firms are not yet insured. The protections are also varied across sectors. Much as how banks were among the first to information share and adapt other best cybersecurity practices, so too here are other sectors behind; only 5% of US manufacturing firms have cyber insurance.

As Elana Broitman explores in her New America report on the needs of a cyber-legislative agenda, Congress can aid in building personal, corporate and national cybersecurity by injecting more life into this marketplace. We are certainly not at the point yet in the debate to where such insurance should be required of all firms, the way fire insurance or car insurance is. However, in lieu of regulation, Congress can push forward key measures to enable better and more flexible market solutions for cybersecurity. It should 1) *hold a series of hearings to better understand the cyber insurance field and its relationship to US national security* 2) *commission a study to explore how DoD buying power and partnerships with the corporate sector, not just in the traditional Defense Industrial Base, but also through Transportation Commands' relationships with broader parts of the economy, can incentivize or require the spread of cyber insurance that would bolster market solutions to raising US national cybersecurity* 3) *help establish an Insurance Laboratory within the National Institute of Standards and Technology (NIST) cybersecurity process,* 4) *work with the industry and state partners to build legislation that would aid in the building of common cybersecurity insurance industry terms and language, something that requires regulatory cooperation across states, thus fitting with Congress's constitutional role; and* 5) *explore the passage of a Cybersecurity equivalent to the Terrorism Risk Insurance cap (TRIA).* Just as such legislation was designed to encourage best practices in protecting infrastructure from conventional terrorism threats post 9-11, the same kind of back stop against catastrophic cyber attacks against critical infrastructure sector (particularly from states in the event of war) would help encourage the spread of insurance that would, not so ironically, help make cyber attacks both less painful and less likely.

The challenge in building true cybersecurity resilience is not only about software and legal code, however, but also about people. This is where there is concern on the new administration's cybersecurity executive order draft. The question is not just what is in it, but what is not; the last drafts to circulate online were lacking any strategic effort to solve our cybersecurity workforce challenges.

Across government and industry, there is a growing lack of cybersecurity professionals; the consultancy Frost and Sullivan estimates that the global gap between security openings and skilled people to fill them will reach 1.5 million by 2020. Thus, even when positions are created and funded, they are difficult to fill, both in private industry and in government. For example, at last report, 40% of the cybersecurity positions at the Federal Bureau of Investigation (FBI) remained unfilled, leaving many field offices without expertise. Diversity is also a problem; less than 10 percent of cybersecurity professionals are women, lower than the already dismal rates in the broader IT world. How can we fill key gaps if we are only recruiting well from less than half the population?

The prior administration created a "Cybersecurity Human Resources Strategy," that should serve as the basis of a move forward. *Congress should oversight implementation of (or not) of the strategy's identifying human resources milestones and aid in building greater resilience by targeting any gaps with scholarship programs and other incentives. The Congress should also task the Department of Education to report on where it can best aid states and cities (where education policy sits in the US) to start to develop genuinely effective cybersecurity education and workforce strategies to fill needed national, state, and local gaps, as well as steer students towards this valuable and well-paying field.*

Filling the human resources pipeline to aiding our cybersecurity is a long term challenge. Of immediate concern, though, is the impact of the Executive Branch's federal hiring freeze on filling needed cybersecurity positions. This has been described as causing "disarray" in areas that range from the US CyberCorps, the scholarship program the serves as a ROTC like feeder for cybersecurity positions (Students are unclear if they can no longer be hired and meet their scholarship obligations) to filling needed IT/cybersecurity positions at agencies that range across the government, from OPM to Treasury (one official said there will soon be "hell to pay" in its near and longterm effect). *Congress should make clear to the Executive branch that cybersecurity related positions, across the federal government, should be excluded from the hiring freeze, given the critical nature of the field and the higher costs that would come from security breaches, nullifying any purported budget savings.*

Any human resources strategy, however, will fail if it only puts new people in old organizational boxes, using the same pipelines.

Attracting more talented civilian expertise into the government though new channels will be a key to supporting a "deterrence by denial" strategy across our broader networks. Consider, for instance, that after the embarrassment of the healthcare.gov rollout, the government created a Digital Service to bring young Silicon Valley innovators into government to do things like fix the federal health care website design and aid the VA in building user-friendly apps. Even after the OPM debacle, however, there is still not a parallel one to shore up cybersecurity. One approach is to simply *expand the USDS to include cybersecurity recruiting as part of a larger extension of the program to 2026.* Additionally, as Adam Segal of the Council on Foreign Relations has recommended, *a cyber version of the Epidemic Intelligence Service (EIS) at the Center for Disease Control and Prevention (CDC) should be established.* The goal in both would be to provide government with a flexible pool of in-house talent and expertise that can aid in training, preventing, and mitigating breaches.

Another area where Congress can aid, importantly in a manner that cuts across traditional partisan lines, is to jumpstart more best practices that bring together the public and private sector. A good illustration is the Pentagon's adaption of a "bug bounty" program. This is a program used by many top companies that offers small rewards to encourage a "crowd sourced" solution to cybersecurity; in essence, it enlists the ingenuity of citizens in the open marketplace to find the holes in our security before the bad guys do. The Pentagon's pilot program offered rewards ranged from $100 to $15,000 for a person that identified multiple security gaps. The experiment with this approach has been a success. Its first bug reports came in just 13 minutes after the contest started. After just 1 month, 1410 outside hackers had submitted 1189 reports to help to spot and fix vulnerabilities in the Pentagon's websites.

The cost was $150,000, an order of magnitude at least cheaper than if the task had been contracted out. But the gains of the program were also about identifying and building out ties to cybersecurity talent beyond government. For example, one of the hackers who helped defend our military's IT systems via this program was a teenager who did helped protect the Pentagon during his high school AP exams. *Congress could play a powerful role in aiding and encouraging the spread of such "bug bounty" programs to each DoD agency, as well as to other federal government agencies. It should also create incentives for similar programs across state and local government partners and private industry.*

Similarly, innovations are needed in our military organizational models. Several National Guard units have been retasked to focus on cybersecurity. They have performed admirably, even besting some active duty Cyber Command units in wargames. But the new units are not enough, nor can they ever be enough. They only serve as a means to organize talent *already* serving in the military. There is a far deeper and wider pool of talent outside the military that is simply not going to be accessed by this effort, either because the individuals are unwilling to meet the various obligations that come with military service (an IT tech in the National Guard, for example, is still legally obligated to serve in any mission they are ordered to, whether it be a cyber 911, Haiti Earthquake response, or Iraq war) or because they are unable to meet the various physical or legal requirements for joining the military.

Here again, there are lessons to be learned from the past that are not usually part of our present day cyber deterrence discussions. During the Cold War, nations like Switzerland or China chose an "active defense" model that was based on deterring attack not by massive retaliation but by mobilizing their citizenry for broader national defense. The United States was in a far different position in the Cold War and so this model was not an apt one for us in the nuclear age.

Today, in the new issue of cybersecurity, there is much to learn from others, past and present, as they wrestle with similar problems. Estonia's Cyber Defense League, for example, is a particularly good model. Rather than a traditional military reserve, it is a mechanism for Estonian citizens to volunteer their expertise for cybersecurity. It is made up of a security-vetted volunteers, who aid the government in everything from "red teaming" --finding vulnerabilities in systems and activities before the bad guys can exploit them-- to serving as rapid response teams to cyberattacks. Notably, the members are not just technical experts, as the needed expertise that lies outside of government is about far more than just computer coding. For example, to defend the national banking system from cyberattack, a mix of hackers and bankers is better than just bankers or hackers.

These efforts have helped turn Estonia from one of the first victims of a state-level cyberattack, when Russian hackers partially shut down the country in 2007, to now being perhaps the best-equipped nation in the world to weather cyber threats. Estonia may not have the same capabilities as the NSA and Cyber Command, but it does have deterrence by denial and an involved populace -- giving it arguably better cybersecurity than the United States.

While the "Minutemen" from the Revolutionary Era is the historic US parallel to Estonia's approach, today, the most apt parallel today would be the U.S. Civil Air Patrol-Air Force Auxiliary, where citizens can build up their own aviation skills, but also volunteer to aid government in anything from aviation-related emergencies to training exercises. The CAP also serves as a useful recruitment and feeder program for future US military pilots. *The Congress should establish a US cybersecurity parallel program to the Estonia's Cyber Defense League and U.S. Civil Air Patrol-Air Force Auxiliary, designed to draw upon our nation's wider technology talent and sense of volunteerism.*

The Special Cases of Elections and Social Media

The success of Russia's attacks on the 2016 election are dangerous not just because of their past impact, but also how they will serve as a guidepost to others in the future. Contrary to the approach so far, however, we must recognize that the critical infrastructure of elections is not just the voting machines, but also the wider ecosystem, including national parties and campaigns. Notably, these groups began to physical security protection from the Secret Service after threats to candidates had both national political relevance and were beyond the private resources of the day (Pinkertons and friends).

Much as banks compete, but still share threat information, our election systems and political organizations, including even both the RNC and DNC, should have had the structures to cooperate in this space; indeed, all that would have been needed to stop the entire DNC hack was a better line of communication with the FBI agents who had been tracking the Russian hacking for years. *Beyond just voting machines and voter databases, Congress should redefine the institutions involved in our democracy as a whole as critical infrastructure, in order to provide higher levels of resourcing and support from the federal government and enable better information sharing.*

More broadly, the 2016 elections point to how we need to understand that the internet is changing. The rise of social media has turned any user into both a collector and sharer of information. It has provided more transparency and engagement, but also means that cyber attacks have pivoted from being merely about controlling computer networks to enabling information warfare. The hacking of a computer system is often now merely the entry point to hacking hearts and minds. A way to think about it is that the Russian efforts to influence the 2016 US election were less like past state-linked hacks of political campaigns in 2008 and 2012, or attacks like those on the OPM. Instead, their parallels were more like the attacks on Sony or the cheaters' website AshleyMadison. These attacks involved not merely the stealing of information, but the outing of it in a manner designed to influence.

Thus, our need for resilience also must extend beyond bits and bytes to building up better political resistance to the influence and information warfare operations that allows Russia and other future attackers to exploit such cyber attacks. We must continue to uphold our freedom of speech, but ensure that authoritarian leaders don't take advantage of it. *Congress should recreate the <u>Active Measures Working Group</u>*, an interagency effort during the Cold War that debunked the worst of Soviet misinformation. In addition, as Secretary Mattis <u>recently noted at the NATO conference</u>, there is "very little doubt" that Russia is targeting for interference "a number of elections in the democracies." It should also *hold hearings on how the United States can better work in cohesion with our NATO allies to help identify and counter Russia's election influence campaigns* (many of which have just pivoted from targeting US to <u>European voters</u>). Importantly, these lines of activity to identify and push back against such campaigns will not just counter outside influencers, but also help in debunking the <u>individuals</u> and outlets who have chosen to become either willing partners or полезные дураки, "useful idiots," for spreading conspiracy theories and foreign government propaganda.

The shift towards social media also connects to a broader lesson: <u>information is being weaponized in new ways</u>. In warfare, social media is not merely an issue for public affairs officers. Just as political campaigns have shifted to reflect the new landscape in their voter outreach, many of our armed adversaries have radically reoriented how they use and integrate social media into everything from their recruiting and propaganda to their intelligence and even conventional military operations. The rise of ISIS and the Russian military operations in Ukraine are exemplars, but the model is now global. In turn, it points to how we have to integrate the same. *Congress should request a report on how the Department of Defense can better utilize and integrate social media into our own training environments, intelligence gathering, and operational planning.*

We also need to better understand not just how social media is being used in conflict, but how it contributes to the very risks of conflict. The change dynamics here range from leader statements that reveal negotiating psychology to those that inflame relations with either adversaries or even with longstanding allies.

This is not just about understanding leaders' personal social media use, but how it shapes the environment around them. Just as newspapers and television once shaped public opinion, and governments had to understand this dynamic, so now does social media. It can empower leaders, but maybe box them in, including even in authoritarian states, such as high levels of nationalism and social media use in China.

It has become a cliché among international-relations scholars to draw parallels to 1914 Europe, but the potential challenges posed by social media make the comparison apt. Then, as now, regimes toyed with the new communications mediums, in order to bolster their standing, which had the effect of amplifying the power of nationalism. These leaders discovered too late that the popular forces they sought to manipulate were beyond their control. *The Congress should request of the intelligence community a briefing on how social media is shaping conflict likelihood and where the Congress can aid in better US capability to understand and monitor this changing force.*

Conclusions

History will record that in 2016 the United States was the victim of the most important cyber attack so far in history. It will judge us by whether and how we respond.

Akin to the Cold War, we face a long-term challenge that has to be managed and mitigated. For as long as we use the Internet, adversaries like Putin's Russia and many others will seek to exploit this technology and our dependence on it in realms that range from politics and business to warfare itself. In response, the United States can build a new set of approaches designed to deliver true cybersecurity, aiming to protect ourselves better, while reshaping adversary attitudes and options. Or, we can keep on talking tough and simple, and continue to be a victim.

Peter Warren Singer
Strategist and Senior Fellow
New America Foundation

The author of multiple award-winning books, he is considered one of the world's leading experts on 21st century security issues. He has been named by the Smithsonian Institution-National Portrait Gallery as one of the 100 leading innovators in the nation, by Defense News as one of the 100 most influential people in defense issues, and by Foreign Policy magazine to their Top 100 Global Thinkers List. His books include Corporate Warriors: The Rise of the Privatized Military Industry, Children at War, Wired for War: The Robotics Revolution and Conflict in the 21st Century. His most recent book is Cybersecurity and Cyberwar: What Everyone Needs to Know, which was named to both the US Army and US Navy professional reading list.

Singer is a contributing editor at Popular Science magazine and the founder of NeoLuddite, a technology advisory firm. He has worked as a consultant for the US military, Defense Intelligence Agency, and FBI, as well as advised a wide-range of technology and entertainment programs, including for Warner Brothers, Dreamworks, Universal, HBO, and the video game series Call of Duty, the best-selling entertainment project in history. He is a member of the US State Department's Advisory Committee on International Communications and Information Policy. His past work included serving as coordinator of the Obama-08 campaign's defense policy task force, in the Balkans Task Force at the Office of the Secretary of Defense, and as the founding director of the Center for 21st Century Security and Intelligence at The Brookings Institution, where he was the youngest person named senior fellow in its 100 year history.

PUBLICATIONS
The wars that come after wars (II): How one can start, or fuel, another one
Article | Sep 9, 2014 | Foreign Policy

The War Of Zeros And Ones
Article | Jul 29, 2014 | Popular Science

For Sale: A New Chinese Tank-Killer? | Popular Science
Article | Jul 10, 2014 | Popular Science

PRESS
Welcome to the Future of War project!
In the News Item | Sep 5, 2014 | Just Security

A CDC for the Internet could help cut down on misbehavior | Washington Post
In the News Item | Aug 22, 2014 | Washington Post

1914-2014: Weapons of the Next Great War
In the News Item | Aug 1, 2014 | US News

U.S. Military Sends Scouting Party Into the Twitterverse | TIME
In the News Item | Jul 10, 2014 | Time

U.S. Military Turns to Hollywood to Outfit the Soldier of the Future | Wall Street Journal
In the News Item | Jul 4, 2014 | Wall Street Journal

It Takes More than Offensive Capability to Have an Effective Cyberdeterrence Posture
Dr. Martin C. Libicki

Testimony before the House Committee on Armed Services
Cyber Warfare in the 21st Century: Threats, Challenges and Opportunities

01 March 2017

The views expressed here are those of the author alone. They do not represent the estimates or policies of the U.S. Navy or any other organization of the U.S. government.

Good morning, Chairman Thornberry, Ranking Member Smith, and distinguished members of the committee. My name is Martin Libicki; I hold the Maryellen and Richard Keyser Chair of Cybersecurity Studies at the U.S. Naval Academy, and am also adjunct management scientist at the non-partisan, non-profit RAND Corporation. The following represents my own viewpoint and not the viewpoint of the U.S. Naval Academy, the Federal Government, or the RAND Corporation.

I thank you for the opportunity to testify today about some issues associated with deterrence of cyberattacks.

Two years ago, the Commander of the US Cyber Command argued in Congressional testimony that he needed a greater ability to conduct offensive cyber operations, stating that its purpose was to be able to deter cyberattacks on the United States.[1]

Clearly, greater capability would not hurt – but would it help much, must less suffice to achieve deterrence?

A successful posture of deterrence – that is, the use of threats to compel others to restrain themselves – has many prerequisites. Four of them merit note. First, the United States has to be able to *attribute* cyberattacks in order to punish the correct party and convince others that the United States is acting justifiably. Second, the United States needs to communicate its *thresholds* – that is, what actions will lead to reprisals. *Third*, U.S. promises to retaliate need *credibility* – so that others believe that punishment will, in fact, follow crossing such thresholds. *Fourth*, the United States needs the *capability* to carry out reprisals.

There are also other considerations but they are not prerequisites, as such. *One* is that carrying out reprisals affects the *broader* relationship between the United States and the attacking country; there may be larger issues in the ongoing relationship which may modulate or exacerbate the reprisal – which in turn affects the credibility and even legitimacy of the

---

[1] "How do we increase our capacity on the offensive side to get to that point of deterrence?"; Ellen Nakashima, "Cyber chief: Efforts to deter attacks against the U.S. are not working," *Washington Post*, March 19, 2015, http://www.washingtonpost.com/world/national-security/head-of-cyber-command-us-may-need-to-boost-offensive-cyber-powers/2015/03/19/1ad79a34-ce4e-11e4-a2a7-9517a3a70506_story.html.

threat. For instance, however annoying the Iranian DDOS attacks on U.S. banks were in late 2012, efforts to halt Iran's nuclear program clearly had higher priority: thus, had reprisals been on the table, their impact on such efforts had to be taken into account. *Two* is the extent to which the attacker feels justified in its original cyberattack (which may have been prompted by something perceived in its past). This, in turn, will color its view of how legitimate the U.S. reprisal is – which, in turn, may influence the likelihood of its making counter-reprisals.

Returning to the prerequisites, the U.S. *capability* to retaliate in cyberspace is least in doubt amongst the four (even if United States need not respond in kind, Admiral Rogers' argument assumed that we needed to be able to do so). Any country credited with Stuxnet and the ability to penetrate systems using techniques described by Ed Snowden has demonstrated a very impressive capability. Whether or not the credit is deserved[2] is secondary. As long as other countries believe we can do magic, what we can *actually* do matters less for deterrence purposes. That noted, however, countries vary in their susceptibility to reprisals in cyberspace. North Korea is a good example because a combination of its economic primitiveness and paranoia about the outside world means that computers and connectivity are far less important to the national well-being than it is in other countries. Note that susceptibility consideration had only a modest effect on the efficacy of the nuclear deterrent. Furthermore, while the U.S. attention to the laws of armed conflict (specifically *jus in bello*) is laudable, the effect of following them is to take certain targets off the list. Such prohibitions are larger if people are worried that cyberattacks on some targets may yield unacceptable collateral damage. Lastly, for those who believe that reprisals delayed are reprisals denied, note that even a very capable United States is limited in its ability to respond from a cyberattack from a country that it did not previously consider a threat and thus whose systems it did not scope in advance. Otherwise, U.S. capability is more than sufficient for purposes of reprisals.

The other three prerequisites are what hobble the ability to develop a coherent deterrence policy.

Attribution, to be fair, has improved considerably over the past ten years. There are several reasons why. Roughly a decade ago, difficulties in attribution were recognized as an important barrier to establishing a deterrence posture. Considerable time and attention was therefore invested in improving the intelligence and science behind attribution; by late 2012, the Secretary of Defense was able to claim that two-thirds of all incidents could be traced back. Furthermore, several private cybersecurity companies – starting most publicly with Mandiant[3] in early 2013 – started making their own attribution claims; this allowed the U.S. Government to make a case against other countries without having to reveal its own sources and methods

---

[2] In the last year, Israel has publicly declared that it and the United States together authored Stuxnet. "Deterring Terror: English Translation of the Official Strategy of the Israel Defense Forces," Belfer Center Special Report of August 2016; http://www.belfercenter.org/publication/israeli-defense-forces-defense-doctrine-english-translation. p. 48.

[3] Mandiant, *APT1: Exposing One of China's Cyber Espionage Units*; sintelreport.mandiant.com/Mandiant_APT1_Report.pdf, March 2013

(even if some government officials believe private attribution claims force their hands when the evidence is less-than-overwhelming or decisions on reprisals need time to make correctly). Although the consonance between what the intelligence community knew and what the private cybersecurity claimed is less than perfect, the two efforts remain quite complementary. It is quite plausible that China's perception that the U.S. ability to attribute acts of economic cyberespionage to the Chinese was good enough sufficed to inhibit further economic espionage from that country after the Xi-Obama agreement to foreswear such activity.

Nevertheless, a few cautions are in order.

First, the ability to attribute and the ability to evade attribution are a measure-countermeasure game. Until the consequences of being caught are severe enough, it may simply not pay for hackers to hide their origins (as opposed to their tracks) very well. Yet, if the point of having a deterrence policy is to inhibit cyberattacks, then presumably consequences have to be severe. If the prospects of reprisals are daunting enough, hackers can be expected to take pains to keep from getting *caught* carrying out cyberattacks. Hence countermeasures to attribution can be expected. Another way of putting it is that attribution will be good until it becomes useful at which point it will cease being good.

Second, the U.S. Government has made less progress in *explaining* why it believes its attribution is correct. After the Sony attack, the FBI's publicly released statement on North Korean attribution devoted just 140 words to justifying its conclusion.[4] The public justification of Russian attribution for the DNC hack is even more problematic. The two public documents released on the matter – one by DHS[5] and the other by the DNI[6] – were generally deemed far from satisfactory. Granted, it may not be obvious why the United States has to convince others that it is right about attribution; by this argument, as long as the attacker knows that it could get caught and punished for what it did – and knows it did – then the opinion of third parties is irrelevant. But is it? To skeptics, U.S. retaliation against a country that could be innocent may strike them not as punishment but aggression. Worse, if potential attackers come to believe that innocence is no guarantee against reprisals, what is the point of being innocent? The accused country could easily maintain its innocence, and having done so credibly (for lack of a good case against it), could justify its responding to retaliation as if it were responding to unprovoked aggression. Thus, what started as an attempt to make other countries conform to standards of responsible behavior becomes an exchange of tit for tat where no one can easily claim the high ground.

---

[4] FBI, "Update on Sony Investigation ," December 17, 2014, http://www.fbi.gov/news/pressrel/press-releases/update-on-sony-investigation

[5] NCCIC, FBI, "GRIZZLY STEPPE – Russian Malicious Cyber Activity," December 29, 2016; https://www.us-cert.gov/sites/default/files/publications/JAR_16-20296A_GRIZZLY%20STEPPE-2016-1229.pdf.

[6] Office of the Director of National Intelligence, "Background to "Assessing Russian Activities and Intentions in Recent US Elections": The Analytic Process and Cyber Incident Attribution," January 6, 2017; https://www.dni.gov/files/documents/ICA_2017_01.pdf.

Credibility also remains an issue when it comes to *cyber* deterrence. Put simply, the United States has yet to retaliate to any cyberattack with any truly serious consequences of the sort that the rest of the world can see.

The U.S. retaliation against North Korea involved sanctions on a handful of individuals. The only quasi-serious response-like event was a DDOS attack on North Korea's thin Internet connection to the rest of the world – and, the United States, if anything, distanced itself from taking credit for that act.[7] There are reports that the United States carried out reprisals against North Korea that did not make the news; although I have no way of evaluating that claim, suffice it to say that hidden reprisals lack effectiveness in persuading *other countries* of the folly of carrying out cyberattacks on the United States.

The United States also retaliated against Russia for the DNC hack by increasing some sanctions and throwing some Russian diplomats out of the country; there may have also been reprisals not visible to the public. Since the Russians probably believe that their contribution to defeating a presidential candidate they disliked exceeded the pain of having to replace a few diplomats, it is difficult to see how the consideration of future such punishment would deter them. Does anyone think the Russians will hereafter refrain from injecting itself into other countries' elections? And what does it say for the credibility of the U.S. Government when representatives of an incoming administration delegitimize the reprisals levied by an outgoing administration?

After two weak *public* responses, the credibility of U.S. reprisals cannot be ranked very high. Perhaps the failure to respond with anything harsher may have been wise given the relatively limited harm associated with both the Sony hack and the DNC hack – and the possibility that a major confrontation would have raised much higher levels of risk. But it would now take a serious response to raise the credibility of a *possible* U.S. response off the floor where it now sits – and several serious responses to convert the possibility into a likelihood. These hypothetical responses to as-yet-potential cyberattacks would carry their own risks. Put another way; if the United States wanted to achieve credibility for a cyberspace deterrence policy, the costs of doing so would not be small at this point.

That leaves *thresholds*, which I want to focus on in part because it seems to get the least attention. Here is the relevant question: what cyberattacks merit cranking up the machinery of U.S. retaliation for? The term, "machinery," is deliberately meant: the decision on whether and how to retaliate would certainly involve the President and the National Security Council, and would have to be followed up by policy adjustments throughout the bureaucracies to reconcile retaliation with whatever else is taking place vis-à-vis the attacking country. Retaliation, after

---

[7] See Nicole Perlroth and David Sanger, "North Korea Loses Its Link to the Internet," December 22, 2014; https://www.nytimes.com/2014/12/23/world/asia/attack-is-suspected-as-north-korean-internet-collapses.html. But two weeks later, sanctions were described as a "first response" suggesting that the DDOS attack was not a U.S. response (BBC, "Sony cyber-attack: North Korea faces new US sanctions," January 3, 2015; http://www.bbc.com/news/world-us-canada-30661973.

all, is an unfriendly act. By contrast, foreign individuals can be indicted in U.S. court – as multiple cybercriminals are – based on decisions taken at the level of a U.S. district attorney and without much reference to the U.S. relationship with the country of their origin. Although the indictment of five members of China's PLA and seven Iranian nationals doubtless required greater coordination, these moves were, at least, announced by someone no higher than an Assistant Attorney General.

The need for a threshold is obvious. Objectionable acts in cyberspace range greatly from a network hiccup to a major catastrophe. Not all of them merit Presidential attention. By contrast, in the nuclear realm, even the detonation of the smallest nuclear weapons on, say, U.S. soil was always going to be an enormous deal.

Finding a tractable and defensible threshold is, alas, a problem not easily solved. Let's consider some candidates that have been bruited about.

Perhaps something is actionable if it violates the U.S. Computer Fraud and Abuse Act. Three problems arise. *First,* using a national law as a red line sets a precedent that can be easily abused by countries whose laws criminalize behavior that is acceptable, even normal, in the United States: e.g., posting on the Internet material critical of the government. In other words, if we use our domestic laws as a basis for international reprisals what keeps others from using their domestic laws in the same way? *Second,* the CFAA is being violated literally millions of times – notably every time a computer is infected as part of an effort to build a botnet, or every time some teenager wants to go exploring in someone else's machine. *Third,* such a law makes cyberespionage generally actionable when the United States relies on such techniques to protect itself from terrorists and hostile countries. Another good reason not to establish a threshold that makes all cyber-espionage actionable is that penetrations can often go undetected for months or years and sometimes forever – whereas the effects of cyberattack in terms of the disruption of operations or the corruption of information is harder to hide. The less likely a violation is to be caught the more problematic it is to punish violations that are.

Another alternative threshold is to use some metric of size to determine whether something is actionable. As one Assistant Secretary of Defense has argued, the United States cares primarily about the top two percent of all cyberattacks.[8] The problem with that formulation is that the criterion for membership in the set of cyberattacks has no obvious lower bound. Two percent of something unmeasurable is itself unmeasurable. Insofar as the effects of cyberattack can almost always be measured in terms of dollars, an economic threshold might make sense – until it comes time to measure impacts. If Sony's statement to the SEC is indicative, the attack from North Korea cost only $35 million (in the financial quarter that took place plus the quarter afterwards). Yet, there are reasons to believe that many intangible costs (e.g., to the reputation of Sony's executives, the hassle of shifting communications from e-mail

---

[8] David Sanger, "Pentagon Announces New Strategy for Cyberwarfare," *New York Times,* April 23, 2015, http://www.nytimes.com/2015/04/24/us/politics/pentagon-announces-new-cyberwarfare-strategy.

to phones, anxiety among employees) were not well captured by that metric. Furthermore, the Administration defended its decision to respond to the Sony attacks and the DNC attacks not by using economic criteria but because such cyberattacks violated transcendent values. That is, the attack on Sony contravened its freedom of speech, while the attack on the DNC contravened U.S. political sovereignty. Meanwhile, there was no U.S. response to the Iranian attack on Las Vegas Sands Corporation, which wreaked damage approximately as large as those suffered by Sony.

Another criterion for judging a cyberattack actionable is if it hurts some part of the U.S. critical infrastructure. One would think such a threshold had sufficient clarity, since the key elements of that infrastructure had been publicly enumerated by DHS (admittedly in response to physical terrorism, which generates a somewhat different list than a focus on cyberspace would). But following the attacks on Sony and the DNC, some have tried to stretch the definition to include such attacks. There were desultory attempts to note that, technically, Sony Entertainment was part of the U.S. critical infrastructure but they were not taken seriously.[9] The DNC hack, however, did persuade the Government to declare the U.S. election system to be critical infrastructure, and properly so.

Perhaps a criterion is needed that offers a parallel with physical attack. Perhaps then, something is actionable if it violates the Laws of Armed Conflict (specifically *jus ad bellum*). LOAC has the benefit of being established international law. But the various laws of armed conflict, having been established for physical combat, focuses on destruction and injury. They do not cover economic loss from hostile activity (perhaps because one country can make many types of decisions that cost other countries money without using force at all). In the decades-long history of cyberwar physical destruction has occurred twice: Stuxnet, and a putative Russian cyberattack on a German blast furnace (in many other cases information was altered that resulted in making machines unusable until reformatted, but that is not physical destruction).[10] No one has yet been harmed as a direct consequence of a cyberattack. Instead, the effects of cyberattacks are usually felt in terms of lost time, hence productivity: e.g., when systems are down or when the data they hold has to be recovered. It is unclear whether an attack that, say, bankrupts a trading house would be actionable by such criteria – and a willingness to declare it so after the fact is not a basis for deterrence.

To complicate matters further, the reliance on precedents such as LOAC fosters the notion that cyberattack, like physical attack, is actionable while cyber-espionage like pre-cyber espionage is acceptable behavior for countries. But accepting *all* cyberespionage as acceptable state behavior is *not* U.S. policy. The United States successfully pressed China to stop its economically-motivated cyberespionage – and by so doing established a norm that was

---

[9] Kim Zetter, "Hacker Lexicon: What Counts as a Nation's Critical Infrastructure?," February 16, 2016; https://www.wired.com/2016/02/hacker-lexicon-what-counts-as-a-nations-critical-infrastructure/.
[10] Kim Zetter, A Cyberattack Has Caused Confirmed Physical Damage for the Second Time Ever" January 8, 2015; http://www.wired.com/2015/01/german-steel-mill-hack-destruction/.

adopted by the G20,[11] which, given the G20's membership, thereby makes it close to a universal norm. If the information taken from OPM had been sold into the black market – the possibility of which was implied by OPMs offering credit-monitoring services to potential victims – then it is quite plausible that the United States would have strongly objected that the acceptability of cyber-espionage did not imply the acceptability of every use of what was taken. Fortunately, there is scant evidence that such information was transferred to criminals. Lastly, it helps to remember that the DNC hack was actually cyberespionage – the results of which would not have led to a U.S. response if the Russians had kept what they took to themselves, rather than use it to influence the outcome of a Presidential election.

These three examples may not be the only occasions where cyberespionage rises to the point where it is as obnoxious as cyberattack. It is characteristic of cyberspace operations that it is very difficult to distinguish between cyberespionage against a system and the preparations made for a cyberattack on such systems. In some cases, the motivation for cyberespionage is so plausible, that countries caught penetrating systems with valuable information can be assumed to have done so out of interest in the information it held than in taking down the system that holds it. But it may be hard to give others the benefit of the doubt when they are caught carrying out cyberespionage against certain elements of a country's critical infrastructure – notably the machine control systems associated with transportation, energy production and distribution, or manufacturing in general – because the information such systems contain is of modest value while the potential for mischief is substantial. Here, too, certain types of cyberespionage may be plausibly deemed actionable if detected, characterized, and attributed.

In the face of these many issues, ensuring that countries do not convince themselves that there is a threshold below which that they can operate with impunity entails deliberately maintaining a threshold so low that the United States can afford to be indifferent to cyberattacks that fall beneath that level. This is hardly a panacea. First, it forces inordinate attention to above-threshold, even if low-level attacks, because the failure to respond to them erodes credibility associated with a U.S. promise to respond (although for some observers, the failure to respond will only erode their belief that the stated threshold is the real one). Second, if there is no difference between the responses to low-level and high-level attacks, potential attackers may reason that if they are going to get caught and punished (again, no sure prospect) they might as well try to achieve a greater rather than a lesser effect. Third, too low a threshold coupled with a fixed minimum cost associated with cranking up the retaliation machinery may strike others as disproportional, expensive, and even arbitrary.

A broader issue in all this is whether any country, even the world's most powerful, can arbitrarily establish redlines as opposed to first achieving some consensus on norms and then

---

[11] For a copy of the communique and a discussion thereof see Cody Poplin, "Cyber Sections of the Latest G20 Leaders' Communiqué," November 17, 2015; https://www.lawfareblog.com/cyber-sections-latest-g20-leaders-communiqué.

using the violation of such norms as a basis for deterrence. To be fair, redlines are not the worst option; at least they have the advantage of needing to be declared beforehand. One of the problems with responding to the DNC hack – apart from its inherently political nature – was that few anticipated that the United States would need to declare against other countries hacking political organizations, extracting their contents of their e-mail, and posting them online. To react to injury solely after the fact assumes that a reasonable presumption could have been made by the attacker that something so injurious could not go unanswered. Such thinking is far from easy even in the physical domain where precedents to almost every conceivable action abound. In the cyber domain, such precedents are absent and the best one can resort to are inexact analogies between something that has merited objection in the past and some objectionable act in the present. Deterrence, after all, only works when the potential attacker knows *in advance* where the redlines are, at least approximately. A country's willingness to respond based on *post facto* redlines presupposes the willingness of others to give the aggrieved country a wide berth.

Redlines have had their place in U.S. history; the Monroe Doctrine which stated the U.S. intolerance for any establishment of new colonies in the Americas could not possibly have been a norm. It was geographically delimited to one hemisphere and the prevailing norm in those days actually allowed colonization in general. Russia's concern over activities in its near abroad, or China's concern over activities within its self-defined first island chain, to use less justifiable examples, are also geographically defined. But cyberspace, as oft observed, does not have the same geography and, to an important extent, has no geography at all. Thus, redlines cannot be stated in geophysical terms very easily – and thus also, a major justification for redlines in order to defend the *physical* basis for a country's sovereignty does not apply.

Redlines and norms differ in several key respects. A country can establish redlines without having to abide by them; when a country establishes exclusion zones for others, it hardly signals its intention to exclude itself. But a norm implies mutual constraint. Every UN member, by dint of its membership, has pledged adherence to norms against carrying out an armed attack on others. Clearly, redlines are less constraining than norms – but that may be exactly why arbitrary redlines sit poorly with long-standing U.S. ideals.

At issue is how rules should govern the world. Until the mid-20th century, international relations could be said to be taken from Thucydides' Melian Dialogue: the strong do as they will and the weak suffer what they must. Redlines bespeak a world in which strong countries – and the United States is the strongest – can set the rules that they can compel others to live by even if they have no intention of living by such rules themselves. But U.S. leadership in the post-war era allowed a different notion to take root. International stability and world peace result when everyone follows the rules, just as domestic stability and safety follow when everyone obeys the law. To achieve legitimacy, that meant that the United States and its friends had to obey the same laws. And much of the history of the Cold War was an attempt – one that was largely successful – to define these laws and use the muscle of the United States and its allies to see that such laws were largely obeyed. The end of the Cold War made that task easier and spread the rule of law wider, but the effort remains non-trivial.

This theoretical difference has a practical consideration. Reconsider the OPM hack. Should the United States have responded? The attack transferred information of great value to China. It embarrassed the U.S. Government. U.S. officials were angry at the Chinese, and there is evidence that Chinese officials were at least somewhat abashed at having been associated with the hack (they subsequently announced an arrest for having carried out the hack[12]). But the DNI and a former CIA director admitted that what the Chinese did was something that the United States would have done if it could have (and it may well have done similar things).[13] The United States could easily declare that it would regard a repeat as having crossed a red line; it might even be able to enforce its dictum. But if the United States would not foreswear doing likewise, it could not argue that a repeat would have violated a norm. One of the reasons that the United States could persuade China to abjure economic cyber-espionage is that it could make a reasonable case that this was behavior that the United States would not conduct – and, indeed, had not conducted (or at least no one has proved the contrary). By the same token, one of the difficulties of dealing with Russia's politically-motivated cyberespionage-cum-doxing was the lack of a norm that made it easy to argue that such activity was out of bounds. Because countries, even the United States, seek to influence the elections of other countries all the time, mere unwarranted influence is a poor guide to norms-writing – but a norm condemning the use of cyberespionage coupled with doxing (for political ends) would be more precise and consistent with U.S. behavior.

A norms-based deterrence posture has its issues. One is determining how much of a consensus is required to establish a norm. One advantage of working from the UN charter is that UN membership is universal – but the conversion from the words of the charter into the new fields of cyberspace is hardly obvious. The European Convention on Cybercrime (aka the Budapest Convention) counts almost every advanced country as a signatory, but Russia, for one, is not a signatory. Treating, say, the Russian's providing sanctuary for major cybercriminals as an actionable violation of universal norms is an iffy proposition. Conversely, waiting until North Korea signs up to norms before deeming them universal means waiting indefinitely. A

---

[12] Ellen Nakashima, "Chinese government has arrested hackers it says breached OPM database" Washington Post, December 2, 2015; https://www.washingtonpost.com/world/national-security/chinese-government-has-arrested-hackers-suspected-of-breaching-opm-database/2015/12/02/0295b918-990c-11e5-8917-653b65c809eb_story.html.

[13] "Don't blame the Chinese for the OPM hack," former NSA and CIA Director Michael Hayden said, arguing that he "would not have thought twice" about seizing similar information from China if he had the chance. (Matthew Ferraro, "On the OPM Hack, Don't Let China Off the Hook," The Diplomat, July 14, 2015,). Director of National Intelligence James Clapper echoed the sentiment, saying at a conference, "you have to kind of salute the Chinese for what they did. . . . If we had the opportunity to do that [to them], I don't think we'd hesitate for a minute."(Jim Sciutto, "Director of National Intelligence blames China for OPM hack," June 25, 2015; http://www.cnn.com/2015/06/25/politics/james-clapper-china-opm-hacking/.).

best guess is that a norm can be deemed universal if it wins adherence from either Russia or China. The other issue is holding others to norms. A country that has declared a redline has put the onus on itself – and only itself – to respond to a redline's violation. Responding to a norms violation, however, is a collective responsibility – which is both good and bad: good, because many countries joint together in responding, and bad because each country can shift the responsibility to the other. In the past, it has fallen to the United States to enforce norms of international behavior, picking up other countries as active allies or passive supporters as their politics dictated. But it is fair to note that despite the lip service that the United States pays to its mutual-defense alliances, it is more likely to react to a cyberattack on itself than to an ally. The best indicator comes from comparing its response to the Sony attack to its non-response to a longer series of more damaging incursions into South Korean systems.

Conclusions

Using the threat reprisals to dissuade cyberattacks introduces multiple issues that need far more careful attention than they have received to date. The notion that building an offensive capability second to none suffices for deterrence is simplistic, to say the least. Granted, weak countries cannot deter, and in there is a basis for Admiral Rogers's argument. But the United States is by no means weak, especially in cyberspace. If the U.S. deterrence policy has problems they are not ones of weakness but wisdom, notably in determining where to draw the line between cyberattacks that are actionable at the national level and those that can either be ignored or responded to via judicial processes.

In the interim, we should understand that there are certain potential cyberattacks – e.g., one that plunges the country into a blackout – that clearly cannot go unanswered, while there are other ones that are simply too trivial to bother with. It is the in-between that is the problem. As a general rule, it would seem appropriate for the United States develop its thresholds by working towards a regime of norms with which the difference between the actions of foreign governments that are acceptable and those that are unacceptable and actionable can be made consistent.

I appreciate the opportunity to discuss this important topic, and I look forward to your questions.

Martin C. Libicki
Adjunct Management Scientist; Professor, Pardee RAND Graduate School

Education
Ph.D. in economics, University of California, Berkeley; M.A. in city and regional planning, University of California, Berkeley; S.B. in mathematics, Massachusetts Institute of Technology

Martin Libicki is an adjunct management scientist at the RAND Corporation, a professor at the Pardee RAND Graduate School, and a Distinguished Visiting Professor at the U.S. Naval Academy. His research focuses on the impacts of information technology on domestic and national security. This work is documented in commercially published books-e.g., Cyberspace in Peace and War (Naval Institute Press, forthcoming), Conquest in Cyberspace: National Security and Information Warfare (Cambridge University Press, 2007) and Information Technology Standards: Quest for the Common Byte (Digital Press, 1995)-as well as in numerous monographs, notably Getting to Yes with China in Cyberspace (with Scott Harold, 2016), Defender's Dilemma (2015), Hackers Wanted (2014), How Insurgencies End (with Ben Connable, 2010), and Cyberdeterrence and Cyberwar (2009). How Terrorist Groups End: Lessons for Countering al Qa'ida (with Seth G. Jones, 2008), Exploring Terrorist Targeting Preferences (with Peter Chalk and Melanie W. Sisson, 2007), and Who Runs What in the Global Information Grid (2000).

His most recent research involved net assessments of Russia and China in cyberspace; modeling cybersecurity decisions, cyberwar strategy, demographic change, and organizing the U.S. Air Force for cyberwar; exploiting cell phones in counterinsurgency; developing a post-9/11 information technology strategy for the U.S. Department of Justice; and using biometrics for identity management.

Prior to joining RAND, Libicki spent 12 years at the National Defense University, three years on the Navy staff as program sponsor for industrial preparedness, and three years as a policy analyst for the U.S. General Accounting Office's Energy and Minerals Division. Libicki received his Ph.D. in city and regional planning from the University of California, Berkeley, writing on industrial economics.

Testimony of

Jason Healey

Columbia University's School Of International and Public Affairs

Saltzman Institute of War and Peace Studies

Before the

United States House of Representatives

Committee on Armed Services

Hearing on

"Cyber Warfare in the 21st Century: Threats, Challenges, and Opportunities"

1 March 2017

Testimony of Jason Healey

Chairman Thornberry, Ranking Member Smith, and distinguished Members of the Committee, thank you for the honor of testifying before you today on the topic of cyber conflict. I am humbled to be here before you today on a topic of such importance.

Our adversaries will continue to use cyber means to challenge American power and our citizens, as it offers significant opportunities for our adversaries, as will be clear from this selection of quotes.

A pioneering expert, Dr. Cliff Stoll, who started his cybersecurity work at one of our national labs, has noted that "[e]spionage over networks can be cost-efficient, offer nearly immediate results, and target specific locations … [while the perpetrators are] insulated from risks of internationally embarrassing incidents," and "the almost obsessive persistence of serious penetrators is astonishing."[1]

This persistence has certainly been clear when it comes to cyber espionage. The National Counter Intelligence Center reported to Congress that "the largest portion of economic and industrial information lost by US corporations" is due to "computer intrusions, telecommunications targeting and intercept, and private-sector encryption weaknesses."[2] Previous testimony to the House of Representatives has furthermore made it clear that "[g]overnment and commercial computer systems are so poorly protected today they can essentially be considered defenseless - an Electronic Pearl Harbor waiting to happen."[3]

Cyber threats are real and getting worse every year, but they are not as new as we think. Each of the previous quotes were made about 25 years ago, if not longer. We have been warning about an electronic Pearl Harbor for 25 of the 75 years since the actual Pearl Harbor; there is a good chance we don't understand the dynamics of cyber conflict as much as we think.

I was the action officer at Headquarters Air Force to help stand up the first joint cyber warfighting command, the Joint Task Force - Computer Network Defense in 1998 and was one of the initial cadre of twenty-five officers. In that time, the central questions and concerns have remained largely the same, even as the risks have grown immeasurably.

---

[1] Dr Cliff Stoll, "Stalking the Wily Hacker," 1988, http://pdf.textfiles.com/academics/wilyhacker.pdf.
[2] NACIC Counterintelligence Report to Congress, July 1995, https://fas.org/sgp/othergov/indust.html.
[3] Winn Schwartau, testimony to House Committee on Science, Space, and Technology, 27 June 1991, https://babel.hathitrust.org/cgi/pt?id=pst.000018472172.

Adversaries

America's adversaries in cyberspace and their motivations are no different than in the physical world: Russia acts because it *lost*, China because it is *behind*, Iran because it is *revolutionary*, North Korea because it is *starving*, and terrorists because they *hate*.

Russia to a large degree remains driven by having lost the Cold War, trying to carve out a sphere of influence in its near abroad and working to undermine the transatlantic victors, the United States, Europe, and the NATO structure that unites both. Since annexing Crimea, Russian cyber operations have gone from quiet, professional political and military espionage to far more aggressive and obvious intelligence and influence operations.

China feels preyed upon by Western powers since the unequal treaties of the mid-1800s. Because China has been unfairly kept down by the West, they believe, anything is permitted to catch back up. For most of the past fifteen years, this meant widespread and aggressive espionage for commercial purposes. It now seems that such espionage has fallen off dramatically, at least in part because of a 2015 agreement by President Obama and President Xi.[4] Should relations with China become more troubled, such as over trade or the South China Sea, we should expect a fresh bout of troublemaking.

Iran continues to see itself as a revolutionary power and this extends into cyberspace as well. Of America's adversaries, Iran has been the most persistent conducting disruptive attacks meant to disrupt US companies and infrastructure, especially banks. Fortunately, as with China, the larger improving diplomatic situation with the United States has helped to throttle back the worst offenses. Since the nuclear agreement was signed, Iranian behavior is reported to be less disruptive, instead focusing on traditional political and military intelligence. Should the deal unwind, Iran would almost certainly act out using a wide range of means, including cyber disruption.

North Korea is starving, both in the literal sense of being poor as well as feeling starved of attention. Cyber capabilities, such that used against Sony Motion Pictures, is a way for the North Koreans to actualize their tantrums as well as have a direct, though limited, impact in South Korea and United States. North Korea knows it cannot keep pace with American and South Korean military capabilities, so cyber sabotage offers unique benefits, as does cybercrime to raise hard currency. Even so, their behavior often closely matches the overall diplomatic environment. Whenever Pyongyang walks away from Panmunjom or has fresh sanctions slapped on it, expect a cyber outburst.

Terrorists would not hesitate to use cyber capabilities if it offered an easy way to act out their hatred. Fortunately, terrorist groups have so far been more of a target of US cyber capabilities than a source of significant attacks. One reason is that it has been historically easy to take down

---

[4] For example, see the FireEye report, "Red Line Drawn," June 2016, https://www.fireeye.com/content/dam/fireeye-www/current-threats/pdfs/rpt-china-espionage.pdf and comments by John Carlin confirming the change in "U.S. Cyber Deal With China Is Reducing Hacking, Official Says," 28 June 2016, https://www.bloomberg.com/news/articles/2016-06-28/u-s-cyber-deal-with-china-is-reducing-hacking-official-says.

a target in cyberspace but hard to keep it down in the face of determined defenses which imposes a relatively high threshold which remain beyond what terrorists can build (or buy). A cyber takedown of France's TV5 appeared to be the beginning of serious cyber terrorism but was, in fact, Russian government hackers.[5]

Defense and Deterrence

With respect to traditional concepts of defense and deterrence, five issues stand out: what isn't a problem, how do we respond, what's most different, what we didn't see coming, and what we might most have wrong. I'm pleased to say that my colleague Professor Robert Jervis and I have been selected for a grant to further study these issues by the Minerva program of the Department of Defense.

What isn't a problem? Attribution is not nearly the challenge anymore that it used to be. Analysts at cybersecurity companies like CrowdStrike and FireEye as well in the US government have made tremendous gains if determining – relatively quickly and with high confidence – what nations are responsible for cyber attacks. As my colleague at Columbia University, Professor Steve Bellovin, points out, analysts have a deep "knowledge base and continuity of contact" spanning over a decade. The remaining challenge is having enough releasable information to convince a skeptical public and having an effective set of policy responses against the nation responsible.

How do we respond? I am also not terribly concerned that the US government has not stated more clearly what might constitute an act of war in cyberspace. Even though we have worried about a Pearl Harbor scenario for 25 years, no nations have used cyber capabilities to kill Americans or to cause destruction or more than even momentary disruption. It seems clear they understand that boundary. Moreover, since 2003, the last two administrations have used varying degrees of clarity to state that the President can respond to cyber incidents with any means of national power.[6]

Moreover, defining forbidden behavior is, in cyber conflict, often an unproductive errand as cyberspace offers adversaries so many possibilities. Neither the North Korean attack on Sony nor the Russian influencing of our elections crossed any of norms proposed, after much consideration, by Secretary of State John Kerry in 2015, nor those agreed to by the G-20 later that year. And unless the United States is unwilling to forego our own gray zone activities, adversaries will not be minded to back down.

We dithered for 10 years before even mentioning to the Chinese we were upset over their commercial cyber espionage. Without options for more effective and timely response, any definitions or red lines are perhaps beside the point. Response requires good enough attribution, which we have achieved, as well as the right policy tools, where more can be done. Most

---

[5] Gordon Corera, "How France's TV5 was almost destroyed by 'Russian hackers'," BBC, 10 October 2016, http://www.bbc.com/news/technology-37590375.

[6] Most notably, in the National Strategy to Secure Cyberspace (2003) and International Strategy for Cyberspace (2011) which both had declaratory statements.

importantly, we need to think more deeply about how our adversaries may try to attack us, develop response playbooks for such eventualities, and to create muscle memory by frequently exercising against these possibilities. Without this agility born of preparation, adversaries will bob and weave in and out of our definitions and red lines.

What's different compared to more conventional conflict? In other testimony, you have surely heard that cyber operations are different because they are at "network speed," or operate across borders, or are so easily denied. Those things are all true, but as Putin showed us by suddenly seizing Crimea with his little green men, they are just as true in other kinds of modern warfare.

No, what is most different is in cyber defense, the private sector is the *supported* command, not the *supporting* command.

America's cyber power is not focused at Fort Meade with NSA and US Cyber Command. The center of US cyber power is instead in Silicon Valley, in Route 128 in Boston, in Redmond, Washington and in all of your districts where Americans are creating and maintain cyberspace and filling it with content the world is demanding. Our critical infrastructure companies are on the front lines of nation state attacks and our cybersecurity companies collectively have even more capabilities to defeat these threats than our military, and can do so at no cost to the public purse and with no arguments over Title 10 versus Title 50 authorities.

The government needs to better support the private sector, not try to force their compliance or deputize them to act out orders coming from the Department of Defense, Department of Homeland Security, or the White House.

Cybersecurity companies, key vendors, and many critical infrastructure companies have unique strengths: agility, subject matter expertise, and the ability to directly change cyberspace in the face of attack. These companies (as well as key non-profit and volunteer groups) are on the commanding heights of cyberspace and are already engaged in keeping it safe. Government bureaucracies cannot easily match any of these capabilities, but can bring massive resources, staying power, and additional authorities, from sanctions to arrest powers to kinetic response. The best hope for American cyber defense is to combine these strengths, not try to re-create them all at Fort Meade.

What didn't we see coming? In the wake of the 1991 Gulf War, the armed services were eager to study and dominate influence operations, so we all studied OODA loops and looked for leverage across any and all information disciplines, from public affairs, civil affairs and counter propaganda to cyber operations and electronic warfare. Even weather prediction was folded into the information operations mix.

The Sony attack and Russian release of DNC documents, the incidents which have had the most immediate national impacts, were not "cyber" as such, but influence operations. Since 2003 or so, we have been so enamored of "cyber", of sending bits and bytes downrange for espionage or to create military effects, we've largely forgotten how to respond to what is now our adversaries' chief weapon. The US military would have been far better prepared to respond to these 20 years ago than today. Putin has not forgotten about information operations, much to the detriment of the United States, Ukraine, and the rest of Europe.

What we might most have wrong? Deterrence remains the most poorly understood dynamic of cyber conflict, with many practitioners and theorists arguing either that it is either not working or altogether impossible. Neither of those is a complete answer, but more worryingly deterrence may be the answer to the wrong question.

Remember that the cyber establishment has been fretting about an electronic Pearl Harbor for twenty-five years. That means for twenty-five years our throats have been strategically bare to our adversaries' attacks and, assumedly, their throats have been vulnerable to ours. Yet, to my research, no one has yet died from a cyber attack. This suggests that nations are in fact showing considerable restraint, at least above the threshold of attacks which might spark a devastating response.

Cyber deterrence, above the threshold of attacks that cause death or physical destruction, not just is working, but works just like more traditional deterrence. This situation might be quiet fragile, as I will explain shortly, and believe that maintaining *stability*, reinforce the threshold below death and destruction, ought to be a higher US priority than seeking deterrence.

Where deterrence is not working, is below that threshold of death and destruction. In this grey area between peace and war, all major cyber powers – the United States included – is enjoying a free-for-all which is getting worse every year. Developments in cyber conflict are driven less by new technologies then the increasing and incredible audacity of the major cyber powers to ever more escalatory activities.

Whenever you hear a US military or intelligence official discussing the need for deterrence, it turns out they often actually mean supremacy. We want to stop the Russians, Chinese, Iranians, and North Koreans from using their cyber capabilities against us, but do not want any notable restraints on use of our grey-zone capabilities against them. Compare this to the Cold War, where we wanted a nuclear edge against the Soviets, but not so that we could actually *use* those capabilities.

Indeed, I suspect cyberspace is the most escalatory kind of conflict that humanity has ever come across. My colleague, Professor Bob Jervis, argued many years ago that escalation was "doubly dangerous" if the offense is dominant over defense and it is hard to distinguish offense from defense.[7] Arms races were especially likely and "incentives to strike first could turn crises into wars."

Unfortunately, the cyber domain not only is distinguished by those two characteristics of offense dominance over defense and difficulty of distinguishing the two. Cyber conflict is far more

---

[7] Robert Jervis, "Cooperation Under the Security Dilemma." *World Politics*. 1978; 30(2): 167-214, https://www.jstor.org/stable/2009958?seq=1#page_scan_tab_contents.

escalatory as it is also hard to distinguish offense from either intelligence collection or intelligence preparation of the battlefield. Cyber conflict also has a low barrier to entry and capabilities are not just stockpiled (as with nuclear or conventional weapons) but actually *used* in unattributed, covert, grey-zone attacks. Cyberspace may not just be "doubly dangerous" but perhaps "quintuply dangerous" and ripe for escalation and miscalculation.

If the United States actively pursues cyber deterrence by ever-greater offensive capabilities and larger, more-capable organizations, other nations can easily respond. Our expenditures and attempts to prevail may only make us less secure.

Worse, there is actually very little evidence of adversaries being deterred by an opponent's fearsome cyber capabilities. But there are many examples, especially between the United States and Iran, where capabilities and operations have led to escalation. Each nation experiences a cyber outrage from the other, which is then used to ratchet up capabilities and operations, which are then used by the other nation to itself ratchet up.

I do not mean to excuse their actions, but when you hear testimony from officials that they need more resources to deal with the Iranian cyber threat, please keep in mind that in cyberspace we threw the first punch. Deterrence works very differently if your adversary is certain they are striking back, not first.

Any exercise in US cyber deterrence is best thought of as an *experiment*. As it turns out, with China the experiment of indictments and threat of sanctions seems to have been more successful than anyone imagined. We cannot take as faith that if only the United States would act in a certain way, such as by pouring money into offensive capabilities or brandishing the awesome US cyber arsenal, that adversaries will be deterred on what, to them, may be a critical national interest.

Please be very skeptical in the face of certainty, even unanimity, of officers or officials about these points. Acting more forcefully, with escalating attacks, may just be pouring gas on a fire, which will affect our Internet-enabled economy far more than our adversaries. As the examples of China and Iran seem to show us, there are other options.

Recommendations

My first recommendation is that the United States takes further steps to deal with foreign influence. Treating these as "cyber" events misses what makes them unique and brings the wrong set of experts to the table. Frankly, we would have better equipped to handle these challenges in the 1990s when forward-looking officers created doctrines, organizations, and operating concepts around information operations, not just cyber.

Even though the military are not the best choice of government agency to respond to other nations seeking to influence or undermine the US system of government, their capabilities might be built up most quickly. The Cyber Mission Force already has area-studies specialists working alongside with cyber subject matter experts. A new set of Cyber Influence Teams could be trained and folded into this structure to provide a more integrated capability to deal with influence events.

Second, I continue to advocate splitting the leadership of NSA and US Cyber Command as soon as possible. The most obvious reason is that two large bureaucracies is one too many for anyone, even our most senior officers to manage well. But other issues bother me even more deeply.

Having intelligence collection and offensive/defensive operations run by the same leader is certainly more efficient and undoubtedly leads to more success for each. Yet if cyber conflict is as escalatory I fear, then some friction between separate leaders is actually a good thing, tamping down escalatory pressures and furthering stability.

I am also concerned that the Pentagon's defensive experts are compromised by being so closely tied to offense and intelligence collection. Since our true cyber power is the private sector, America's defenses will be most effective and responsive not if we work to optimize the relationship between NSA and Cyber Command but rather between government and those key private sector firms. This means reducing classification, creating a clear dividing line between NSA and US Cyber Command, and within NSA, preserving the independence of the Information Assurance Division. The Department of Defense has some of the crown jewels of America's cyber defense, but without these steps like this, they will continue to be seen as compromised in the eyes of the technology community, just another part of the agencies "weaponizing" vulnerabilities in their software.

Perhaps an analogy can help. Imagine the commander of U.S. Pacific Command were the leading source of information on the Chinese military threat, was active in all NSC meetings on China policy, ran the best-funded China-oriented bureaucracies, was involved in covert military operations against China, and could decide what information on China was classified. Americans, with centuries-old traditions of mistrust, would never accept such a concentration of power and yet this is what we've intentionally constructed in the dual-hat arrangement. Two heads – and two hats – are better than one.

Third, since the private sector is the supported command, the best use of government resources is to reinforce those doing the best work. Cybersecurity companies and other key parts of the private sector are already fully engaged with America's adversaries in cyberspace, so the government should be hesitant to try to imitate their agility, subject matter expertise, or ability to directly measure and change and change cyberspace.

As another analogy, there are many, many players on the cyber ballfield. Odds are, the player most able to make the play is a private-sector entity. Cyber defense is weakened if one player, the government, constantly runs around the entire field, yelling "I've got it, I've got it!" Maybe those other players can't see the ball clearly, or need a better glove or need practice drills to get better at playing their position. Maybe indeed they don't even know they are playing the game. But bringing them up to speed is far cheaper and more effective than hiring more bureaucrats or diverting an already limited number of military personnel.

Grants are perhaps the most obvious example of how this could be done. At one point, the non-profit Financial Services Information Sharing and Analysis Center, of which I used to be vice-chairman, would only share threat information and best practices with the 50 or so companies which were dues-paying members. The Department of the Treasury helped us out of this sub-optimal situation with a grant of $2 million to upgrade the technology and expand sharing to all thirteen-thousand plus banks and credit unions in the nation. Now the FS-ISAC is widely recognized as the model for security and information sharing, making that perhaps the best spent $2 million in US government cyber history. Though this example was for the finance sector, I'm sure examples abound for armed services and national security.

If I were back in the White House, this would my top short-term project. The most comprehensive way to identify such groups is for the executive branch to conduct a review of one or two representative response for each kind of major attack against the United States and the Internet. These could include major denial of service, malware spread (such as Conficker), critical infrastructure attack (such as Iran against the finance sector), botnet takedown, and release of emails (like the DNC or Sony). Such a review, which would only cost a few million dollars, would examine who took what decisions, based on what information, and leading to what actions to alleviate the crisis. This review then could be used to improve national incident response plans, drive information sharing requirements, identify promising partners for the Departments of Defense and Homeland Security, and identify promising new projects for the most national defense at least cost.

Lastly, I'd like to leave you with a questions which I like to ask my colleagues, especially those still serving in uniform or elsewhere in government: *What do you believe will be the dominant form of cyber conflict will be in ten years?*

When, for example, the Air Force Chief of Staff appears before this committee on the need for a Long-Range Strike Bomber, it is because the Air Force's conviction that future air combat will be dominated by the need to operate across very long distances over denied airspace. Yet, in cyberspace the Pentagon seems to have a healthy set of requirements but not the same sense of what future conflict will be like.

Just to list one likely and disruptive possibility, what if in 10 years most cyber conflict is fought between intelligent software bots, constantly changing their forms and backed by powerful supercomputers? We've already tested a nascent version of supercomputer-driven malware, with DARPA's Cyber Grand Challenge. After all, trading in stocks is now dominated by algorithms and human floor traders are largely superfluous. Why is this not a likely future for cyber conflict also and, if so, what are the implications for US Cyber Command staffing and projects and overall US cyber defenses?

In closing, I'd like to address a small part of the cyber workforce talent gap. Five years ago, I helped create the Cyber 9/12 Student Challenge, for university students to tackle exactly the same sort of national security cyber challenges about which my colleagues and I are testifying before you today. The next competition will be held at American University on 16 and 17 March at American University with teams from many of your districts, including the US Air Force Academy, Brown University, the University of South Alabama, and the University of Maryland College Park. I've included the full list of 32 universities sending one of the 48 competing teams as an appendix to my written remarks. If you or your staff are available to observe, judge or provide remarks, I'm sure the student teams would benefit greatly.

Thank you for your time. Mr. Chairman and Members of the Committee, this concludes my testimony.

Healey — Testimony to HASC, 1 March 2017

Appendix: Teams Competing in Cyber 9/12 Student Challenge

16 and 17 March 2017

Organized by the Atlantic Council and hosted at American University

1. Air University
2. American University
3. Arizona State University
4. Brown University
5. Carnegie Mellon University
6. Columbia University
7. Daniel Morgan Graduate School of National Security
8. Duke University
9. Georgetown University
10. Indiana University
11. John Hopkins University
12. Lewis University
13. Marymount University
14. Middlebury Institute of International Studies at Monterrey
15. National Defense University
16. National Intelligence University
17. Stanford University
18. Texas A&M University
19. The George Washington University
20. Tufts University
21. United States Air Force Academy
22. United States Military Academy
23. United States Naval Academy
24. United States Naval War College
25. University of Maine
26. University of Maryland, College Park
27. University of Maryland, Baltimore County
28. University of South Alabama
29. University of South Carolina
30. University of Texas Austin
31. University of Texas El Paso
32. University of Virginia

Jason Healey
Nonresident senior fellow for the Cyber Statecraft Initiative
of the Atlantic Council

Jason Healey is a nonresident senior fellow for the Cyber Statecraft Initiative of the Atlantic Council and senior research scholar at Columbia University's School of International and Public Affairs, focusing on international cooperation, competition, and conflict in cyberspace. From 2011 to 2015, he worked as the director of the Council's Cyber Statecraft Initiative. Under his leadership, the Initiative made its mission "Saving Cyberspace" to help create a more sustainable Internet that remains as open and free for future generations as it was for its pioneers. He guided the Initiative's work with Fortune 500 companies, governments, and other stakeholders to examine the overlap of national security, international relations, and economic security issues and to promote thought leadership in cyber statecraft.

Mr. Healey is also the editor of the first-ever history of cyber conflict, A Fierce Domain: Conflict in Cyberspace, 1986 to 2012 and coauthor of the book Cyber Security Policy Guidebook by Wiley. Additionally, his ideas on cyber topics have been widely published in over a hundred articles and essays published by the Atlantic Council; the National Research Council; academic journals such as those from Brown and Georgetown Universities; along with the Aspen Strategy Group and other think tanks. Mr. Healey is also the president of the Cyber Conflict Studies Association.

Mr. Healey has unique experience working issues of cyber conflict and security spanning fifteen years across the public and private sectors. As director for Cyber Infrastructure Protection at the White House from 2003 to 2005, he helped advise the President and coordinated US efforts to secure US cyberspace and critical infrastructure. He has worked twice for Goldman Sachs, first to anchor their team for responding to cyberattacks and later as an executive director in Hong Kong to manage Asia-wide business continuity and create the bank's regional crisis management capabilities to respond to earthquakes, tsunamis, or terrorist attacks. Immediately after the 9/11 attacks, his efforts as vice chairman of the Financial Services Information Sharing and Analysis Center created bonds between the finance sector and government that remain strong today.

Starting his career in the United States Air Force, Mr. Healey earned two Meritorious Service Medals for his early work in cyber operations at Headquarters Air Force at the Pentagon and as a plankholder (founding member) of the Joint Task Force – Computer Network Defense, the world's first joint cyber warfighting unit. He has degrees from the United States Air Force Academy (political science), Johns Hopkins University (liberal arts), and James Madison University (information security).

QUESTIONS SUBMITTED BY MEMBERS POST HEARING

MARCH 1, 2017

Mr. FRANKS. Background: How are forensics done in a timely manner to determine if the attack was nonstate, state actor, or local terrorist? Once identified by DOD, what authorities are required to conduct a mission to stop the attack, mitigate it in the future, and/or attribution of the origin of the attack.

Question: What is USCYBERCOM doing to counter our adversaries before, during, and after an attack or probe on DOD networks?

Dr. SINGER. There are a wide variety of forensics, some of which involve monitoring your own network activity, other's gaining access to and monitoring potential attacker networks, and even the use of information outside cyberspace (HUMINT for example). The key is to establish awareness of the attack as rapidly as possible which then allows an appropriate response. To some attacks, you might simply want to close off access. Others, you might want to feed them false information. And still others might be an act of war that require response in realms beyond cyberspace.

CYBERCOM engages in and prepares for these range of scenarios. A key, as in my written testimony, is more exercises/wargames that stress test our own systems, explore new doctrines. Better to find vulnerabilities or discover new methods in the practice than in the big game.

Mr. FRANKS. Background: Industrial control system (ICS) is a general term that encompasses several types of control systems and associated instrumentation used in industrial production, including Supervisory Control and Data Acquisition (SCADA) systems, distributed control systems (DCS), and other smaller control system configurations such as programmable logic controllers (PLC) often found in the industrial sectors and critical infrastructures. Since cyber is a man-made domain of operations, DHS should be responsible for ICS/SCADA attacks as they are in industry. However, since cyber happens so fast, attribution can be a challenge to determine if this is really a U.S.C. Title 10, 18, 32 etc... lane of responsibility. So imagine a bomber from a state actor was heading to the U.S. with intent to destroy an oil refinery. Who should respond? DHS or DOD?

Question: Who do you believe is responsible to respond to SCADA/ICS network attacks? If DHS, what is USCYBERCOM or DOD doing to facilitate/support the operations as all data transverses over the same IP provider?

Why would DHS be responsible for defense or counter measure against a state actor, wouldn't DOD be planning those actions?

Dr. SINGER. ICS is used everywhere from U.S. navy ships to traffic lights to energy plants to toymakers. The defense of such systems would be shared across the operators of the systems, supported by legal authorities (DHS etc) and, if moving into the realm of state attack in the context of war, the DOD. For example, DHS and other government agencies can't/shouldn't operate a toymaker or oil refinery's SCADA system on its own, but it should be enabling the operators to better defend themselves in realms that range from information sharing, standards setting, threat intelligence etc, as well as incentivizing the market via insurance etc. In turn, if a state actor did attack such a system with the intent of making war (physical damage etc), we wouldn't want the toy or oil company to retaliate, but the U.S. military and other relevant agencies, with our means not limited to only cyber retaliation.

Mr. FRANKS. Background: Since 1988 each of the theater, unified commands have established a separate Special Operations Command (SOC) to meet its theater- unique special operations requirements. As subordinate unified commands, the theater SOCs provide the planning, preparation, and command and control of SOF from the Army, Navy, and Air Force. They ensure that SOF strategic capabilities are fully employed and that SOF are fully synchronized with conventional military operations, when applicable.

SOCs, established as sub-unified commands of the combatant unified commands, are the geographic Combatant Commander in Chiefs (CINCs) sources of expertise in all areas of special operations, providing the CINCs with a separate element to plan and control the employment of joint SOF in military operations. Additionally, SOCs provide the nucleus for the establishment of a joint special operations task force (JSOTF), when a joint task force is formed. There are six SOCs supporting geographic CINCs worldwide.

Question: If the SOCOM model has worked for years with proven performance in geographic AORs, why hasn't USCYBERCOM moved out to support the warfighter in the same manner?

Dr. SINGER. As a young organization, with a unique positioning vis STRATCOM and NSA, U.S. CYBERCOM has not been structured of empowered to act like a full equivalent of SOCs as you lay out. I do believe that it is evolving towards this model (vs a TRANSCOM-style or separate service future) and Congress would do well to support studies on what aspects of the model are applicable or not, and what challenges that the SOCOM organization has faced (particularly in its cohesion with theater command) might be navigated as CYBERCOM moves forward.

Mr. FRANKS. Background: How are forensics done in a timely manner to determine if the attack was nonstate, state actor, or local terrorist? Once identified by DOD, what authorities are required to conduct a mission to stop the attack, mitigate it in the future, and/or attribution of the origin of the attack.

Question: What is USCYBERCOM doing to counter our adversaries before, during, and after an attack or probe on DOD networks?

Dr. LIBICKI. Attribution is the process of narrowing down who did what. In the United States, it uses a combination of intelligence (apparently, we track certain cyber groups) and forensics. The latter uses information from the attack such as the IP addresses and malware used, social engineering tricks, and nation-linked indicators (such as language)—to make an educated guess about who did it. Much of it is quick; some of it is slow and depends on the flow of future information: e.g., an attack that we know was carried out by X leaves indicators which then match the indicators of an earlier attack which can then be attributed. Some recent trends— notably the use of black-market tools—are troubling for attribution because they could be wielded by anyone.

USCYBERCOM's ability to do anything prior to an attack largely depends on its foreknowledge of particular hacker groups (and would thus be of limited use against an unknown hacker). The best we can hope for—if the hackers themselves are unaffected by whatever the United States does (e.g., are not arrested)—is to be able to postpone an attack and force the group to develop new accesses as well as new tools or techniques. At best, this buys six months (taking down a botnet can provide somewhat longer relief but that's a different form of cyberattack). At worst, the attackers have been dealt a minor inconvenience, and the better hackers have backup plans in case their infrastructure (e.g., their favorite IP sites) are discovered and compromised. *Please note that I have never worked for CYBERCOM, and any statements about them are based on my understanding of unclassified information.

Mr. FRANKS. Background: Industrial control system (ICS) is a general term that encompasses several types of control systems and associated instrumentation used in industrial production, including Supervisory Control and Data Acquisition (SCADA) systems, distributed control systems (DCS), and other smaller control system configurations such as programmable logic controllers (PLC) often found in the industrial sectors and critical infrastructures. Since cyber is a man-made domain of operations, DHS should be responsible for ICS/SCADA attacks as they are in industry. However, since cyber happens so fast, attribution can be a challenge to determine if this is really a U.S.C. Title 10, 18, 32 etc... lane of responsibility. So imagine a bomber from a state actor was heading to the U.S. with intent to destroy an oil refinery. Who should respond? DHS or DOD?

Question: Who do you believe is responsible to respond to SCADA/ICS network attacks? If DHS, what is USCYBERCOM or DOD doing to facilitate/support the operations as all data transverses over the same IP provider?

Why would DHS be responsible for defense or counter measure against a state actor, wouldn't DOD be planning those actions?

Dr. LIBICKI. Everything depends on what the response is. DOD gets the call to prevent bomber aircraft from getting to the refinery because of how bombers are engaged (e.g., with other aircraft, or by anti-aircraft systems). DHS or local police would get the call to prevent a terrorist from getting to the refinery because such a terrorist would be engaged by border enforcement and/or police action. A similar logic would dictate how a hacker would be stopped from attacking SCADA/ICS networks. If the particulars of exploit are understood, it can be stopped by the defensive actions of the network owners; DHS may play a role but only insofar as its advice works and is considered useful and actionable. If the origin but not the particulars of the exploit are understood, it may be possible to block the relevant bytes at the border (or would be if the legal authority existed and the ISPs were equipped to detect and sinkhole the relevant bytes). If the origin or a waypoint of the attack were known but nothing else, there is the possibility of covert action by CYBERCOM or the CIA against the relevant node (although as the last answer indicated, that only buys time and not much. If the author of the exploit were identified but nothing else was known the, author may be subject to police action (especially if the author sat in friendly territory). If the author sat in a hostile country, it may be up to the State Department to persuade the country to yield the individual. If nothing else worked, and there was no other way to head off the attack (and, in fact, there often are many other ways), the author could be militarily attacked but that is tantamount to waging war on another country—which carries risks unless the country is essentially ungoverned or already a war zone (but these are qualities that make it difficult to carry out cyberattacks from such locations).

Mr. FRANKS. Background: Since 1988 each of the theater, unified commands have established a separate Special Operations Command (SOC) to meet its theater- unique special operations requirements. As subordinate unified commands, the theater SOCs provide the planning, preparation, and command and control of SOF from the Army, Navy, and Air Force. They ensure that SOF strategic capabilities are fully employed and that SOF are fully synchronized with conventional military operations, when applicable.

SOCs, established as sub-unified commands of the combatant unified commands, are the geographic Combatant Commander in Chiefs (CINCs) sources of expertise in all areas of special operations, providing the CINCs with a separate element to plan and control the employment of joint SOF in military operations. Additionally, SOCs provide the nucleus for the establishment of a joint special operations task force (JSOTF), when a joint task force is formed. There are six SOCs supporting geographic CINCs worldwide.

Question: If the SOCOM model has worked for years with proven performance in geographic AORs, why hasn't USCYBERCOM moved out to support the warfighter in the same manner?

Dr. LIBICKI. When CYBERCOM started up, its Commander (GEN Alexander) argued that all the forces belonged to him and he would direct their use. Over time the relationship between particular mission teams and the regional CINCs have grown closer to the SOC model. I think that trend is continuing. But there are two reasons why they may never be the same.

First, offensive cyber operations often rely on a bag of tricks (some of which are zero-day exploits). Once these tricks are exposed, they cannot be easily reused. Thus there may have to be some central allocation of these tricks so that high-value tricks are not used for low-value objectives. This use-once feature does not apply to special operations quite so much. Similarly, there is a lot of common learning that has to happen and a unified organization provides a basis for such learning.

Two, getting the requisite access to a target system can take a long time. There is no equivalent of kicking down the door. Thus, teams have to be dedicated to targets well in advance of when these targets are attacked. The bullpen model—here are some forces, what would you like them to do for you today—does not work very well for cyberspace operations.?

Mr. FRANKS. Background: How are forensics done in a timely manner to determine if the attack was nonstate, state actor, or local terrorist? Once identified by DOD, what authorities are required to conduct a mission to stop the attack, mitigate it in the future, and/or attribution of the origin of the attack.

Question: What is USCYBERCOM doing to counter our adversaries before, during, and after an attack or probe on DOD networks?

Mr. HEALEY. I defer to USCYBERCOM for the particulars.

Mr. FRANKS. Background: Industrial control system (ICS) is a general term that encompasses several types of control systems and associated instrumentation used in industrial production, including Supervisory Control and Data Acquisition (SCADA) systems, distributed control systems (DCS), and other smaller control system configurations such as programmable logic controllers (PLC) often found in the industrial sectors and critical infrastructures. Since cyber is a man-made domain of operations, DHS should be responsible for ICS/SCADA attacks as they are in industry. However, since cyber happens so fast, attribution can be a challenge to determine if this is really a U.S.C. Title 10, 18, 32 etc... lane of responsibility. So imagine a bomber from a state actor was heading to the U.S. with intent to destroy an oil refinery. Who should respond? DHS or DOD?

Question: Who do you believe is responsible to respond to SCADA/ICS network attacks? If DHS, what is USCYBERCOM or DOD doing to facilitate/support the operations as all data transverses over the same IP provider?

Why would DHS be responsible for defense or counter measure against a state actor, wouldn't DOD be planning those actions?

Mr. HEALEY. Answer 1: The first response will always be the private sector and only the private sector. Neither DOD nor DHS have any capability to respond in any kind of timely way and neither additional authorities nor money will make any difference.

DHS can help ensure coordination happens and has some role, but it is as a supporting actor, one among many in an ensemble cast, not the leading role.

Answer 2: After the first response, which is only the responsibility of the private sector, then the U.S. government does have more of a role. If it comes to counter measures, then DOD ought to plan and execute those actions.

I recommend each critical infrastructure sector should have one military unit, chosen from the Guard or Reserves, which specializes in that sector and can help this coordination. For example, an Air Guard or Reserve squadron from Texas (where many cyber units are located) could specialize in the oil and gas sector. Another unit, perhaps from the Army Guard or Reserve, could specialize in the finance sector, and work with that sector's organizations, like the Finance Sector Information Sharing and Analysis Center (FS–ISAC).

Mr. FRANKS. Background: Since 1988 each of the theater, unified commands have established a separate Special Operations Command (SOC) to meet its theater- unique special operations requirements. As subordinate unified commands, the theater SOCs provide the planning, preparation, and command and control of SOF from the Army, Navy, and Air Force. They ensure that SOF strategic capabilities are fully employed and that SOF are fully synchronized with conventional military operations, when applicable.

SOCs, established as sub-unified commands of the combatant unified commands, are the geographic Combatant Commander in Chiefs (CINCs) sources of expertise in all areas of special operations, providing the CINCs with a separate element to plan and control the employment of joint SOF in military operations. Additionally, SOCs provide the nucleus for the establishment of a joint special operations task force (JSOTF), when a joint task force is formed. There are six SOCs supporting geographic CINCs worldwide.

Question: If the SOCOM model has worked for years with proven performance in geographic AORs, why hasn't USCYBERCOM moved out to support the warfighter in the same manner?

Mr. HEALEY. My apologies, I am not aware of how USCYBERCOM has organized itself in this regard and the reasons why. I defer to them for the particulars.

————

QUESTIONS SUBMITTED BY MS. HANABUSA

Ms. HANABUSA. When we talk about cyber warfare, naturally, we tend to focus on where the threats are. In the Asia-Pacific, that means China, North Korea, and to a lesser extent, Russia. However, we rarely focus on our allies—nations we can partner with in the cyber domain to build capacity, share information, and mutually defend each other. Can you speak to how we're cooperating with our allies on cyber warfare, particularly Asia-Pacific nations like Japan, South Korea, and Australia?

Dr. SINGER. We have various levels of both information sharing and agreements with our partners in Asia, with Australia having the added link of the ''5 Eyes'' participation. Two key areas to enhance are 1) aligning our norm building, so that it is not each country individually pushing for action by an adversary state, but multilateral and global alliances, and 2) joint military training, as adversaries can/will seek to exploit alliance vulnerabilities and seams.

Ms. HANABUSA. When we talk about cyber warfare, naturally, we tend to focus on where the threats are. In the Asia-Pacific, that means China, North Korea, and to a lesser extent, Russia. However, we rarely focus on our allies—nations we can partner with in the cyber domain to build capacity, share information, and mutually defend each other. Can you speak to how we're cooperating with our allies on cyber warfare, particularly Asia-Pacific nations like Japan, South Korea, and Australia?

Dr. LIBICKI. My best understanding is that there is a lot of interchange among all three Pacific allies, but they are better characterized as from time-to-time rather than day-to-day. As for defense, there is a large and growing world of contractors whose advice is probably as good as and sometimes better than what is available from allies' military forces or other employees. When it comes to offense, however, security classification levels are very high; we probably share a lot more with Australian (a Five-Eyes member) than we do with Japan and South Korea.

Ms. HANABUSA. When we talk about cyber warfare, naturally, we tend to focus on where the threats are. In the Asia-Pacific, that means China, North Korea, and to a lesser extent, Russia. However, we rarely focus on our allies—nations we can partner with in the cyber domain to build capacity, share information, and mutually defend each other. Can you speak to how we're cooperating with our allies on cyber warfare, particularly Asia-Pacific nations like Japan, South Korea, and Australia?

Mr. HEALEY. There are excellent stories to tell here, in quiet diplomacy, sharing, and cooperation with key nations, including those in the Asia-Pacific region. The Departments of Defense, State, and Homeland Security and the DNI can give you more detailed answers, but it is worth noting we've got long-standing signals intelligence relationships with all three of these nations, agreements which have extended into cyber capabilities. In addition, the United States has held extensive bilateral agreements with these countries, in addition to India, and works closely with Singapore. Perhaps more important, U.S. companies work extensively with their subsidiaries and peers in these countries, ensuring that attacks are prevented and stopped, at no cost to governments (and with no arguments about authorities).

––––––

QUESTIONS SUBMITTED BY MS. ROSEN

Ms. ROSEN. Cyberspace has been called the fastest evolving technology space in human history, both in scale and properties. The United States was the victim of great exploitation of this technology realm in the 2016 election, and in your testimony you call it "the most important cyber-attack so far in history." If our cyber systems do not out-perform those of our adversaries, our national power is at risk in all of the domains in which we operate. What specifically must the United States do, that we are not yet addressing, to deter adversaries in this complex threat environment, and how should we respond to those who aim to meddle in it?

Dr. SINGER. In my written testimony I identified 30 specific and non-partisan actions that the Congress could take to better protect the nation. Available at: http://docs.house.gov/meetings/AS/AS00/20170301/105607/HHRG-115-AS00-Wstate-Singer P-20170301.pdf

If we do not better respond to Russia's operations, we undercut any future cyber deterrence.

Ms. ROSEN. Is our cyber force structured for rapid response to meet national requirements and combatant commander needs, or are we mired by the bureaucracy of a NSA and CYBERCOM dual-hat command?

Dr. SINGER. The time has come to establish Cyber Command's long-term status and disentangle the "dual hat" leadership structure with the National Security Agency. These two valuable organizations work in the same realm, but they must reflect different organizational culture, goals, and processes. Of note, among the original rationale for this "dual" structure was concern that the leadership of Cyber Command would not have enough stature with Congress; instead, the post-Snowden debates have meant that Congress has more often become interested in their NSA role.

Ms. ROSEN. How does our cyber apparatus differ from those of our state-adversaries and allies? What technologies are they using and how are they employing them?

Dr. SINGER. There are some 100 plus nations that have cybersecurity organizations of some kind, parallel to the U.S. Cyber Command. They range in their funding, number of personnel, etc. but one of the most noted is how they make use of entities beyond government. The U.S., for instance, tends to rely on private contracting companies, while Russia, as a point of comparison, has made use of criminal networks and China of university linked cyber militia. As I submitted in my testimony, the Estonian model of better leveraging civilian expertise is an apt model for the U.S.

Ms. ROSEN. What additional efforts should we be making to protect against hacking? Do you see an obvious action that Congress should take?

Dr. SINGER. In my written testimony I identified 30 specific and non-partisan actions that the Congress could take to better protect the nation http://docs.house.gov/meetings/AS/AS00/20170301/105607/HHRG-115-AS00-Wstate-SingerP-20170301.pdf

Ms. ROSEN. How is attribution possible without revealing sources and methods of U.S. cyber capabilities?

Dr. SINGER. Full sources and methods will not be able to be disclosed in every case. In some situations, the information will only be able to shared at different levels of clearance or with some information removed. But this should not limit all attribution. A good parallel is the 2011 alleged Iranian plot to conduct an attack inside the U.S. The U.S. government attributed it to Iran but did not disclose ALL our sources and methods. Yet the House still voted for sanctions. As I point out in my testimony, the case of Russia's attacks on U.S. targets is backed by an extensive and wide range of both U.S. government but also private company information. The question now is not whether Russia did it, but how will we respond?

Ms. ROSEN. Is our cyber force structured for rapid response to meet national requirements and combatant commander needs, or are we mired by the bureaucracy of a NSA and CYBERCOM dual-hat command?

Dr. LIBICKI. The primary barrier to a rapid response is not our inability to make decisions so much as it is the difficulty in acquiring and maintaining access to systems that we might want to attack via cyberspace. A large part of the reason that cyberattacks were not used against Libya is that prior to the Arab Spring there was no good reason to penetrate Libyan air defenses to create a capacity for some later cyberattack. Once such a reason existed, there was not enough time to exploit such penetrations for effect before other faster means could be brought to bear.

Ms. ROSEN. What additional efforts should we be making to protect against hacking? Do you see an obvious action that Congress should take?

Dr. LIBICKI. As a general rule, the primary defenses against cyberattack are those undertaken by network/system owners. For non-government systems, the Government is on the outside looking in. It can provide assistance, but cannot guarantee that such assistance will be used (or if used, used effectively). But there are exceptions. 1. Certain systems, notably the electric grid, should be isolated from the outside world (and not just put behind firewalls, many of which are permeable). Furthermore, they should be able to pass penetration tests to indicate they are, in fact, isolated. Legislation to that end, as long as it is temporary (so that the result can be evaluated) and limited to the electric grid (it helps to take one step at a time) could be useful. 2. DDOS attacks are a unique concern. Unlike with most cyberattacks, they do not arise because of something the victims themselves did wrong. ISPs should be given some authority and incentive to detect and sinkhole the traffic that constitutes a DDOS attack—but exactly how is something I'm still wrestling with.

Ms. ROSEN. Is our cyber force structured for rapid response to meet national requirements and combatant commander needs, or are we mired by the bureaucracy of a NSA and CYBERCOM dual-hat command?

Mr. HEALEY. I suspect the answer you get from U.S. Cyber Command is that they want to be escalated so they be better structured for rapid response. This is probably true but certainly overstated.

It is worth noting the DOD first created in 1998 a special joint command with the authorities to counter attacks and probes on DOD networks. It has been therefore nearly 20 years and yet DOD still has similar problems. I'm not convinced elevation to a unified command will resolve these issues any more than the escalation of this from a two-star to three-star command (in 2004), or from three-stars to four (in 2010).

Moreover, some friction is actually beneficial. Cyber conflict is extremely complex, and is fought in, through, and with the products of American technology companies on which we all depend for innovation and prosperity. Attacks can cascade in unpredictable ways. In air warfare, we have learned that if we push the rules of engagement too low, we end up bombing Afghani weddings. We should be similarly careful here.

Further, the use and stockpiling of capabilities can cause outrage in citizens who feel their privacy and trust is being violated. We should be wary of taking away too much of the mire or the Congressional oversight function will be overwhelmed with incidents and complaints.

Ms. ROSEN. Discuss the role of industry in cyber warfare and cyber operations. What is the relationship between the government and these private companies, and privacy?

Mr. HEALEY. Americans seem to trust private sector companies with their information far more than they do the U.S. government. (Note, this tends to be the opposite in Europe.) This can be a strength for cyber defense, as cybersecurity companies tend to have far greater capabilities, and fewer restrictions, than the DOD or DHS.

A smart policy will refocus American cyber defense so the private sector is the supported command, not the supporting command.

Ms. ROSEN. What additional efforts should we be making to protect against hacking? Do you see an obvious action that Congress should take?

Mr. HEALEY. My top practical step for Congress to take is to require DOD and DHS to conduct a review of how the United States has responded to past incidents.

In a structured way, they should look at two of each major kind of attack (countering a denial of service attack, for example, and kicking out foreign spies) to determine which organizations and people took which decisions, based on what information and which led to what effectiveness in mitigating the attack.

The results of this review will suggest how the U.S. government could have better responded better in the past and suggest how to do better in future. This should then be the basis of a new cyber incident response plan.

I suspect an accurate review would show that most of the decisions and actions which have mattered were taken by the private sector, not just the companies under attack, but the software vendors (e.g. Microsoft), network service providers (e.g. AT&T), and cybersecurity companies (e.g. Symantec). Other critical actions are likely to be taken by small non-profits who are critical to sharing and response, such as ISACs (information sharing and analysis centers).

Congress could develop grant programs to help these non-profits, if it proves they could be doing more critical work. This would be far cheaper to the public purse than hiring more DOD bureaucrats. It would also allow far better oversight, as Congress could better see just where the executive branch is succeeding and failing.

O

CyberSecurity Standards Library™

NIST SP 500-288	Specification for WS-Biometric Devices (WS-BD)
NIST SP 500-291 V2	NIST Cloud Computing Standards Roadmap
NIST SP 500-292	NIST Cloud Computing Reference Architecture
NIST SP 500-293 V1 & V2	US Government Cloud Computing Technology Roadmap
NIST SP 500-293 V3	US Government Cloud Computing Technology Roadmap
NIST SP 500-299	NIST Cloud Computing Security Reference Architecture
NIST SP 500-304	Data Format for the Interchange of Fingerprint, Facial & Other Biometric Information
NIST SP 800-1	Bibliography of Selected Computer Security Publications January 1980-October 1989
NIST SP 800-12 R1	An Introduction to Information Security
NIST SP 800-13	Telecommunications Security Guidelines for Telecommunications Management Network
NIST SP 800-14	Generally Accepted Principles and Practices for Securing Information Technology Systems
NIST SP 800-15 V1	Minimum Interoperability Specification for PKI Components (MISPC)
NIST SP 800-16 R1	A Role-Based Model for Federal Information Technology/Cybersecurity Training
NIST SP 800-17	Modes of Operation Validation System (MOVS): Requirements and Procedures
NIST SP 800-18 R1	Developing Security Plans for Federal Information Systems
NIST SP 800-19	Mobile Agent Security
NIST SP 800-20	Modes of Operation Validation System for the Triple Data Encryption Algorithm
NIST SP 800-22 R1a	A Statistical Test Suite for Random and Pseudorandom Number Generators for Cryptographic Applications
NIST SP 800-23	Guidelines to Federal Organizations on Security Assurance and Acquisition/Use of Tested/Evaluated Products
NIST SP 800-24	PBX Vulnerability Analysis - Finding Holes in Your PBX Before Someone Else Does
NIST SP 800-25	Federal Agency Use of Public Key Technology for Digital Signatures and Authentication
NIST SP 800-27 Rev A	Engineering Principles for Information Technology Security (A Baseline for Achieving Security)
NIST SP 800-28	Guidelines on Active Content and Mobile Code
NIST SP 800-29	A Comparison of the Security Requirements for Cryptographic Modules in FIPS 140-1 and FIPS 140-2
NIST SP 800-30	Guide for Conducting Risk Assessments
NIST SP 800-31	Intrusion Detection Systems
NIST SP 800-32	Public Key Technology and the Federal PKI Infrastructure
NIST SP 800-33	Underlying Technical Models for Information Technology Security
NIST SP 800-34 R1	Contingency Planning Guide for Federal Information Systems
NIST SP 800-35	Guide to Information Technology Security Services
NIST SP 800-36	Guide to Selecting Information Technology Security Products
NIST SP 800-37 R2	Applying Risk Management Framework to Federal Information
NIST SP 800-38	Recommendation for Block Cipher Modes of Operation
NIST SP 800-38A Addendum	Block Cipher Modes of Operation: Three Variants of Ciphertext Stealing for CBC Mode
NIST SP 800-38B	Block Cipher Modes of Operation: The CMAC Mode for Authentication
NIST SP 800-38C	Block Cipher Modes of Operation: The CCM Mode for Authentication and Confidentiality
NIST SP 800-38D	Block Cipher Modes of Operation: Galois/Counter Mode (GCM) and GMAC
NIST SP 800-38E	Block Cipher Modes of Operation: The XTS-AES Mode for Confidentiality on Storage Devices
NIST SP 800-38F	Block Cipher Modes of Operation: Methods for Key Wrapping
NIST SP 800-38G	Block Cipher Modes of Operation: Methods for Format-Preserving Encryption
NIST SP 800-39	Managing Information Security Risk
NIST SP 800-40 R3	Guide to Enterprise Patch Management Technologies
NIST SP 800-41	Guidelines on Firewalls and Firewall Policy
NIST SP 800-43	Systems Administration Guidance for Securing Microsoft Windows 2000 Professional System
NIST SP 800-44 V2	Guidelines on Securing Public Web Servers
NIST SP 800-45 V2	Guidelines on Electronic Mail Security
NIST SP 800-46 R2	Guide to Enterprise Telework, Remote Access, and Bring Your Own Device (BYOD) Security
NIST SP 800-47	Security Guide for Interconnecting Information Technology Systems
NIST SP 800-48	Guide to Securing Legacy IEEE 802.11 Wireless Networks
NIST SP 800-49	Federal S/MIME V3 Client Profile
NIST SP 800-50	Building an Information Technology Security Awareness and Training Program
NIST SP 800-51 R1	Guide to Using Vulnerability Naming Schemes
NIST SP 800-52 R1	Guidelines for the Selection, Configuration, and Use of Transport Layer Security (TLS) Implementations
NIST SP 800-53 R5	Security and Privacy Controls for Information Systems and Organizations
NIST SP 800-53A R4	Assessing Security and Privacy Controls
NIST SP 800-54	Border Gateway Protocol Security
NIST SP 800-55 R1	Performance Measurement Guide for Information Security
NIST SP 800-56A R3	Pair-Wise Key-Establishment Schemes Using Discrete Logarithm Cryptography
NIST SP 56B R 1	Recommendation for Pair-Wise Key-Establishment Schemes Using Integer Factorization Cryptography
NIST SP 800-56C R1	Recommendation for Key-Derivation Methods in Key-Establishment Schemes - Draft
NIST SP 800-57 R4	Recommendation for Key Management
NIST SP 800-58	Security Considerations for Voice Over IP Systems
NIST SP 800-59	Guideline for Identifying an Information System as a National Security System
NIST SP 800-60	Guide for Mapping Types of Information and Information Systems to Security Categories
NIST SP 800-61 R2	Computer Security Incident Handling Guide
NIST SP 800-63-3	Digital Identity Guidelines
NIST SP 800-63a	Digital Identity Guidelines - Enrollment and Identity Proofing
NIST SP 800-63b	Digital Identity Guidelines - Authentication and Lifecycle Management
NIST SP 800-63c	Digital Identity Guidelines- Federation and Assertions
NIST SP 800-64 R2	Security Considerations in the System Development Life Cycle

Click on a title to obtain a printed copy of these standards at Amazon.com

CyberSecurity Standards Library^{TM}

Click on a title to obtain a printed copy of these standards at Amazon.com

CyberSecurity Standards Library™

Click on a title to obtain a printed copy of these standards at Amazon.com

CyberSecurity Standards Library^{TM}

NISTIR 7601	Framework for Emergency Response Officials (ERO)
NISTIR 7611	Use of ISO/IEC 24727
NISTIR 7617	Mobile Forensic Reference Materials: A Methodology and Reification
NISTIR 7621 R1	Small Business Information Security: The Fundamentals
NISTIR 7622	Notional Supply Chain Risk Management Practices for Federal Information Systems
NISTIR 7628 R1 Vol 1	Guidelines for Smart Grid Cybersecurity - Architecture, and High-Level Requirements
NISTIR 7628 R1 Vol 2	Guidelines for Smart Grid Cybersecurity - Privacy and the Smart Grid
NISTIR 7628 R1 Vol 3	Guidelines for Smart Grid Cybersecurity - Supportive Analyses and References
NISTIR 7658	Guide to SIMfill Use and Development
NISTIR 7676	Maintaining and Using Key History on Personal Identity Verification (PIV) Cards
NISTIR 7682	Information System Security Best Practices for UOCAVA-Supporting Systems
NISTIR 7692 V2	Specification for the Open Checklist Interactive Language (OCIL)
NISTIR 7693	Specification for Asset Identification 1.1
NISTIR 7694	Specification for the Asset Reporting Format 1.1
NISTIR 7696 V2.3	Common Platform Enumeration: Name Matching Specification
NISTIR 7697 V2.3	Common Platform Enumeration: Dictionary Specification
NISTIR 7698 V2.3	Common Platform Enumeration: Applicability Language Specification
NISTIR 7711	Security Best Practices for the Electronic Transmission of Election Materials for UOCAVA Voters
NISTIR 7756	CAESARS Framework Extension: An Enterprise Continuous Monitoring Technical Refer
NISTIR 7764	Status Report on the Second Round of the SHA-3 Cryptographic Hash Algorithm Competition
NISTIR 7770	Security Considerations for Remote Electronic UOCAVA Voting
NISTIR 7771 V2	Conformance Test Architecture for Biometric Data Interchange Formats - Beta
NISTIR 7773	An Application of Combinatorial Methods to Conformance Testing for Document Object Model Events
NISTIR 7788	Security Risk Analysis of Enterprise Networks Using Probabilistic Attack Graphs
NISTIR 7791	Conformance Test Architecture and Test Suite for ANSI/NIST-ITL 1-2007
NISTIR 7799	Continuous Monitoring Reference Model, Workflow, and Specifications - Draft
NISTIR 7800	Applying the Continuous Monitoring Technical Reference Model to the Asset, Configuration, and Vulnerability Management Domains - Draft
NISTIR 7823	Advanced Metering Infrastructure Smart Meter Upgradeability Test Framework
NISTIR 7874	Guidelines for Access Control System Evaluation Metrics
NISTIR 7904	Trusted Geolocation in the Cloud: Proof of Concept Implementation
NISTIR 7924	Reference Certificate Policy
NISTIR 7987	Policy Machine: Features, Architecture, and Specification
NISTIR 8006	NIST Cloud Computing Forensic Science Challenges
NISTIR 8011 Vol 1	Automation Support for Security Control Assessments
NISTIR 8011 Vol 2	Automation Support for Security Control Assessments
NISTIR 8040	Measuring the Usability and Security of Permuted Passwords on Mobile Platforms
NISTIR 8053	De-Identification of Personal Information
NISTIR 8054	NSTIC Pilots: Catalyzing the Identity Ecosystem
NISTIR 8055	Derived Personal Identity Verification (PIV) Credentials (DPC) Proof of Concept Research
NISTIR 8060	Guidelines for the Creation of Interoperable Software Identification (SWID) Tags
NISTIR 8062	Introduction to Privacy Engineering and Risk Management in Federal Systems
NISTIR 8074 Vol 1 & Vol 2	Strategic U.S. Government Engagement in International Standardization to Achieve U.S. Objectives for Cybersecurity
NISTIR 8080	Usability and Security Considerations for Public Safety Mobile Authentication
NISTIR 8089	An Industrial Control System Cybersecurity Performance Testbed
NISTIR 8112	Attribute Metadata - Draft
NISTIR 8135	Identifying and Categorizing Data Types for Public Safety Mobile Applications
NISTIR 8138	Vulnerability Description Ontology (VDO)
NISTIR 8144	Assessing Threats to Mobile Devices & Infrastructure
NISTIR 8151	Dramatically Reducing Software Vulnerabilities
NISTIR 8170	The Cybersecurity Framework
NISTIR 8176	Security Assurance Requirements for Linux Application Container Deployments
NISTIR 8179	Criticality Analysis Process Model
NISTIR 8183	Cybersecurity Framework Manufacturing Profile
NISTIR 8192	Enhancing Resilience of the Internet and Communications Ecosystem
Whitepaper	Cybersecurity Framework Manufacturing Profile
Whitepaper	NIST Framework for Improving Critical Infrastructure Cybersecurity
Whitepaper	Challenging Security Requirements for US Government Cloud Computing Adoption
FIPS PUBS 140-2	Security Requirements for Cryptographic Modules
FIPS PUBS 140-2 Annex A	Approved Security Functions
FIPS PUBS 140-2 Annex B	Approved Protection Profiles
FIPS PUBS 140-2 Annex C	Approved Random Number Generators
FIPS PUBS 140-2 Annex D	Approved Key Establishment Techniques
FIPS PUBS 180-4	Secure Hash Standard (SHS)
FIPS PUBS 186-4	Digital Signature Standard (DSS)
FIPS PUBS 197	Advanced Encryption Standard (AES)
FIPS PUBS 198-1	The Keyed-Hash Message Authentication Code (HMAC)
FIPS PUBS 199	Standards for Security Categorization of Federal Information and Information Systems
FIPS PUBS 200	Minimum Security Requirements for Federal Information and Information Systems

Click on a title to obtain a printed copy of these standards at Amazon.com

Copyright © 2017 4th Watch Publishing

CyberSecurity Standards Library™

FIPS PUBS 201-2   Personal Identity Verification (PIV) of Federal Employees and Contractors
FIPS PUBS 202   SHA-3 Standard: Permutation-Based Hash and Extendable-Output Functions

DHS Study   DHS Study on Mobile Device Security

OMB A-130 / FISMA OMB A-130/Federal Information Security Modernization Act

DoD
UFC 3-430-11   Boiler Control Systems
UFC 4-010-06   Cybersecurity of Facility-Related Control Systems
FC 4-141-05N   Navy and Marine Corps Industrial Control Systems Monitoring Stations
MIL-HDBK-232A   RED/BLACK Engineering-Installation Guidelines
MIL-HDBK 1195   Radio Frequency Shielded Enclosures
TM 5-601   Supervisory Control and Data Acquisition (SCADA) Systems for C4ISR Facilities
ESTCP   Facility-Related Control Systems Cybersecurity Guideline
ESTCP   Facility-Related Control Systems Ver 4.0
DoD   Self-Assessing Security Vulnerabilities & Risks of Industrial Controls
DoD   Program Manager's Guidebook for Integrating the Cybersecurity Risk Management Framework (RMF) into the System Acquisition Lifecycle
DoD   Advanced Cyber Industrial Control System Tactics, Techniques, and Procedures (ACI TTP)

NERC
NERC CIP 002-5.1 Cyber Security — BES Cyber System Categorization
NERC CIP 003-6   Cyber Security — Security Management Controls
NERC CIP 003-7(i) Cyber Security — Security Management Controls
NERC CIP 004-6   Cyber Security — Personnel & Training
NERC CIP 005-5   Cyber Security — Electronic Security Perimeter(s)
NERC CIP 006-6   Cyber Security — Physical Security of BES Cyber Systems
NERC CIP 007-6   Cyber Security — Systems Security Management
NERC CIP 008-5   Cyber Security — Incident Reporting and Response Planning
NERC CIP 009-6   Cyber Security — Recovery Plans for BES Cyber Systems
NERC CIP 010-2   Cyber Security — Configuration Change Management and Vulnerability
NERC CIP 011-2   Cyber Security — Information Protection
NERC CIP 014-2   Physical Security